INTEGRATION AND PARTICIPATION

Women's Work in the Home
and in the Labour Force

Canadian Advisory Council on the Status of Women

1987

Prepared for the
Canadian Advisory Council on the Status of Women
Box 1541, Station B
Ottawa, Ontario
K1P 5R5

This document expresses the views of the authors and does not necessarily represent the official policy of the CACSW.

Available free of charge from the
Canadian Advisory Council on the Status of Women

Cette publication existe aussi en français.

CONTENTS

PREFACE

This book contains a collection of essays compiled by the Canadian Advisory Council on the Status of Women in keeping with its mandate to "bring before the government and the public matters of interest and concern to women". For the most part, the essays are about money, work, or both — and about how money and work in the home and in the labour force affect women at various stages in their lives.

Eight of the ten chapters in the book review the legal, regulatory, and practical considerations that govern women's economic status and the quality of their working lives, whether they work in the home, in the paid labour force or both. The issues examined include marriage and divorce, conditions of work, unemployment, health and safety, unionization and pensions.

Work on these chapters began four years ago, with the collaboration of Council members and staff and outside contributors. In two areas, recent and rapid change necessitated a fresh look at the implications of these issues for women. These subjects are covered in Chapter Four, which reviews current proposals for reform of the unemployment insurance system, and Chapter Ten, which examines the pension system and recent recommendations to improve the financial security of retired women. These chapters were prepared for the Council by Monica Townson and Ginette Dussault respectively.

The Council wishes to acknowledge the contribution of the many people who participated in preparing this volume. They include current and former Council staff, as well as consultants engaged on contract by the Council. Three chapters are the work of individual authors: Louise Dulude (Chapter Two), Kathryn Running (Chapter Seven) and Karen Stotsky (Chapter Six). Among the contributors to the other chapters are Patty Deline, Margaret Evans, the Participatory Research Group, Craig Paterson, Monica Townson, and Margaret White.

Sylvia Gold
President

CHAPTER ONE

BALANCING A FAMILY AND A JOB

In an economic climate that appears to offer dark clouds but few silver linings, many people are either glad to have a job or desperate to find one. When the major contemporary concern about work is unemployment, other important issues receive less attention. Such issues include the quality of employment, movement toward equal sharing by women and men of housework and child care, and the way time is divided between working for pay and other activities. These questions tend to get pushed to the sidelines, viewed as luxury concerns that can be considered only when economic prosperity permits.

The number of hours spent working for pay, and how these hours are arranged during the day, week, month and year, received a lot of attention in Canada during the 1970s. The introduction of flextime and the compressed work week were heralded as revolutionary concepts for the working day and the working week. Many speculated that such programs were merely the first steps away from the nine-to-five, five-days-a-week employment pattern and that more progressive shifts in the concept of normal employment hours would inevitably follow.

However, as unemployment started to rise, attention shifted to the shrinking job market and the lack of employment for all those who needed it. The time had passed for experimenting with and speculating about new ways of organizing the hours spent in employment in order to increase time for leisure and home life. Concern centred instead on enforced reductions in the hours of employment, the introduction of work-sharing programs as a way of avoiding layoffs, and a concern that part-time jobs would replace full-time jobs, to the detriment of those who needed a full-time paycheque. Today, discussions about hours of work almost invariably take place from the perspective of unemployment and the impact of technological innovations on the availability and hours of employment.

While these considerations require immediate attention, other issues concerning patterns of work time or how work is allocated within couples and families continue to have tremendous effects on the daily life and economic position of women, their spouses and their families. These issues must not take a back seat in times of economic crisis and high unemployment. In fact, they should be a part of decisions about how to deal with unemployment, and they need to be a touchstone in deciding which type of social policy directed at alleviating unemployment would be the most beneficial. In other words, in deciding how best to deal with the problem of unemployment, we must make sure that we move toward, rather than away from, a form of employment that facilitates the equal access of women and men to hours of paid work, to time for childrearing, and to leisure time.

The current debates about full employment and unemployment policies and the effects of technological change are discussed in detail in other chapters of this volume. In this chapter, we focus on the division of labour between paid work and domestic work and how it affects women's economic position. We go on to describe how hours of work vary for women and men and to present alternative ways of organizing the time spent on different types of work.

HOURS OF WORK FOR WOMEN AND MEN

The number of hours a woman works depends on how her time is divided between paid and domestic labour and therefore varies according to her stage of life and social circumstances. On average, single women spend less time working than married women do. Although single women spend almost 15 minutes more per day in paid employment, married women spend more than twice as much time on domestic work (almost 5 hours a day, compared to 2 hours for single women). Consequently, while a single woman averages a work day of 9 hours, the married woman is working more than 11 hours per day.[1]

As would be anticipated, a woman with children spends, on average, less time in the paid labour force than does a woman with no children (six hours, compared to seven hours per day) and more time on domestic labour (five hours, compared to three hours per day). In total, then, a mother spends one hour more per day working than does a woman without children.[2]

It is clear that family responsibilities have an important impact on women's hours of work, which consequently fluctuate over a woman's lifetime. The work required to maintain a household increases when children arrive, and motherhood often means a reduction in the number of hours that women work for pay. To accommodate the increased demands of home and family life, women may withdraw from paid work altogether or move from a full-time to a part-time paid job. In recent years there has been a remarkable increase in labour force participation by mothers with young children, so that 56% of women with pre-school age children were in the labour force in 1985. Still, it remains the case that 44% of women with children under six years old were full-time homemakers, and 22% worked in the labour force part-time.[3]

The latest and most detailed study of the hours of work of husbands and wives is Michelson's research on families in Toronto. It

2

confirms that the degree of participation in the paid labour force has a significant effect on the hours of work of married women with children (Figure 1.1).

Full-time homemakers work, on average, 7¼ hours per day on household and child care tasks. Married women with children and part-time jobs cut back their domestic work to 6 hours per day and spend an average of 2 further hours working for pay, for a total of 8 hours. The married mother with a full-time job has by far the longest working day — almost 9 3/4 hours, despite cutting household chores and child care back to 3¼ hours.[4]

To maintain these working hours, the wife and mother employed full-time cuts back on her leisure and sleep time. She experiences the greatest pressure over her multiple responsibilities, and the greatest tension, while full-time homemakers experience the least difficulty, and part-time workers fall in between. Thirty-seven per cent of mothers with full-time jobs say that they feel a conflict "quite often or very often" between being a mother and having a job, compared to 18% of mothers who are employed part-time. Similarly, only 25% of mothers with full-time employment state that they are very satisfied with the balance between paid work and family, compared to 53% of part-time workers.[5]

Part-time work is a major way for women to bring some income into the family while managing housework and child care responsibilities. One-quarter (26%) of all married women in paid jobs are part-time workers, compared to less than 3% of employed married men.[6] However, part-time work carries a heavy cost. Most part-time work is available only in the clerical, service and sales sectors and at the lowest levels, with rarely any opportunity for change or advancement. This type of work is predominantly low-paid, with few benefits and little security, and the low rate of unionization among part-time workers inhibits improvement in these conditions.[7] Over three-quarters of a million women who are married, divorced, or widowed work part-time.[8] The costs of their reduced employment are not dissimilar to those facing women who withdraw entirely from the labour force for a period: the loss of recognized work experience, the difficulty of re-entering the labour force on a full-time basis, and the lack of protection in the event of sickness, disability, unemployment, and old age, because of the loss of employment-related benefits.

Figure 1.1   Work on a Weekday for Couples with Children under 15

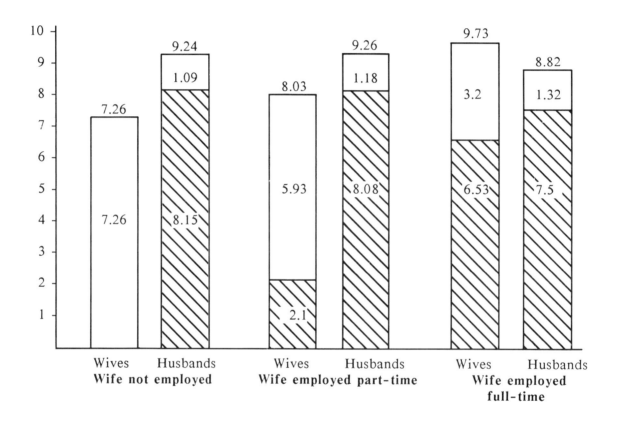

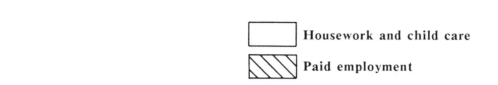

Source: Unpublished data from William Michelson, author of *From Sun To Sun. Daily Obligations and Community Structure in the Lives of Employed Women and their Families* (New Jersey: Rowan and Allanheld, 1985).

Women clearly make the major adjustments in type and hours of work in response to family life, but husbands and fathers do not remain unaffected. When women reduce their hours of paid work to attend to childrearing, they receive little independent financial support for their parenting role, and the family's income falls. Evidence suggests that men increase their hours of paid work to compensate for the loss of the wife's income and to cover the cost of an expanding and financially dependent family.

Time budget studies have found that husbands of full-time homemakers work longer hours in paid jobs than do husbands of women with full-time employment. The difference, illustrated in Figure 1.1, is half an hour per day and has been found to be as much as 3½ hours per week.[9]

In 1985, 31% of men, compared to 12% of women, worked in paid employment for more than 40 hours per week, and 19% of men worked over 50 hours per week.[10] Married men typically work somewhat longer hours than single men. In the childrearing years, between 25 and 44 years of age, married men work an average of 43½ hours per week, compared to 41 hours per week for single men.[11]

Given these long hours of employment, men who are the sole financial support in their families work longer hours of combined paid and domestic work than do their wives, by 2 hours each weekday (Figure 1.1). The gap between husbands and wives is narrowed to less than 1½ hours when the wife is employed part-time. However, where the wife is in full-time employment, the husband's daily hours of paid work drop to 7½ hours, and he works almost an hour less per day than his wife does.

While men's hours of paid work vary, the hours spent by men on housework and child care are remarkably constant. Whether their wives are employed full-time, part-time, or not at all, husbands spend, on average, one hour per day on domestic labour (Figure 1.1).

When children arrive, many women reduce their hours of paid employment, while men may increase their hours on the job, particularly if they are the sole financial support in the household. Domestic labour increases for mothers and remains primarily their responsibility, regardless of their labour force participation. As a result of these adjustments, husbands work longer hours of combined paid and domestic work if their wives are full-time homemakers or employed part-time. However, mothers who are also employed full-time work the longest hours of anyone. The results of these adjustments are

■   an increased divergence in the work done by women and men, as women take on primary responsibility for domestic labour and men remain in the labour force and even increase their hours of paid work;

5

- for mothers who also work full-time, high levels of stress and tension and doubts about the balance of family and employment responsibilities;

- increased financial stress in families where the wife is a full-time homemaker and the financial dependence of these mothers; and

- lack of employment-related benefits — which provide financial security — for full-time homemakers and many part-time workers.

If couples are forced to make these kinds of adjustments, how do single parents cope with the demands upon their time? It is often assumed that their hours of work must be more demanding because there is no partner to share the labour. In fact, this is not the case. For combined paid and domestic work, employed women who are single parents work just over an hour less per weekday than married mothers do (8.6 hours, compared to 9.7 hours). Half an hour less is spent on paid employment, and slightly more than half an hour is gained by reducing the time spent on domestic labour. It should be noted that single mothers who are not employed also spend less time on housework and child care than do married homemakers.[12]

In his work on this question, Michelson has indicated several possible explanations for this unexpected trend. The incomes of single parents are substantially lower than those of married parents, and if the parents own neither a house nor a car, or if the parent's living space is smaller, less time is required in maintenance and cleaning. The single mothers in Michelson's study also averaged fewer children than the married mothers. Since employed married women continue to carry primary responsibility for domestic work, and the contribution from husbands is limited, single parents are not actually deprived of a great deal of help. Moreover, a husband is a source of additional work, insofar as he is another person to be taken care of, requiring his schedule, concerns and tastes to be accommodated. Lastly, single-parent mothers were more likely than married mothers to obtain help with work from their children and from outside sources. Whatever the combination of factors contributing to their fewer hours of work, single-parent mothers report that they experience slightly less time pressure and tension than married mothers report.

Women and men make accommodations for child care and financial support within existing constraints, but there are indications that they do not consider these arrangements satisfactory. More than one study has found that both men and women favour alternatives that would allow each to contribute to parenting and financial maintenance on a more equitable basis.[13] How can this be achieved?

ALTERNATIVE WAYS OF WORKING

There are four major ways of modifying the pattern of paid work:

- compressed time;
- flextime;
- reduced hours of work and part-time work; and
- maternity and parental leave.

Compressed Time

The 40-hour work week has been the norm in Canada since the 1950s. However, two alternative ways to distribute the 40 hours through the week were introduced in the early 1970s: the compressed work week and flextime.

The compressed work week involves working the standard hours of a full-time job in less than five days. Usually, the compressed work week means working 10 hours a day for four days a week, although it may involve three 12-hour shifts, an arrangement that has become common in nursing. In 1974, the Canadian Labour Congress opposed the compressed work week because it "erodes the principle of the 8-hour day", and proposed instead that legislation establish a 32-hour, four-day work week, with no decrease in take-home pay. At the time, the CLC was not concerned about the effect of the compressed work week on women's double workload or an equitable division between parenting and paid work for women and men.

In fact, the compressed work week is not necessarily a progressive transformation of employment in these respects. Because the compressed work week extends the hours of paid work per day, it may exacerbate the problems parents often experience when they work an 8-hour day. At least one study has indicated that, while some women like having an extra day for household tasks, parents have found that the longer working day makes child care more, not less difficult.[14] However, a recent Gallup Poll found that 50% of Canadians supported the idea of working four 10-hour days. Although more women than men continue to prefer the five-day week (53%, compared to 46%), fully 42% of women expressed a preference for the compressed work week.[15] Further research is necessary on the impact of the compressed work week, particularly upon parents and child care.

Flextime

Flextime was also introduced into the Canadian work force in the early 1970s and began on an experimental basis in the public service sector. Basically, flextime involves a distinction between core hours (commonly 9:30 a.m. to 3:30 p.m.) and flexible hours before and after core hours (7:00 a.m. to 9:30 a.m. and 3:30 p.m. to 6:00 p.m.). All employees work core hours but have flexibility in choosing a starting and finishing time within the flexible hours. In other words, employees work standard full-time hours, but they have some flexibility to determine how those hours are spread over the day. More elaborate flextime schedules have also been tried; for example, in some cases employees can bank extra hours for use at a later date.

Although flextime was typically introduced as a way of easing the urban transit problems associated with a nine-to-five work day, it has also been recommended as a means for women to reduce the stress of managing paid work and family responsibilities. It has also been suggested that flextime for men would facilitate increased sharing of domestic responsibilities between husbands and wives. However, a detailed and controlled study of these issues has raised questions about the benefits of flextime.[16] While workers on flextime usually like the arrangement and feel that it gives them increased control over their schedules, flextime workers who are also mothers do not experience less stress than those with standard hours, parents do not spend more time with their children, and husbands on flextime do not help more with household chores. The workers who benefited from flextime in terms of reduced stress were single adults without children, married women without children, and fathers whose wives were not employed, that is, workers without primary responsibility for children. The authors of the study conclude, "Plainly, the magnitude of the logistical, energy and time demands on families with two employed parents, or a single parent, cannot be dramatically altered by minor changes in daily work schedules."[17] Because flextime, like the compressed work week, does not reduce the hours of paid work, the flexibility in flextime is in fact limited.

Perhaps a major benefit from the introduction of the compressed work week and flextime was the dislodging of the idea that a nine-to-five, five-days-a-week work pattern is the only optimal way of organizing the hours spent in paid work. However, unless alternative ways of organizing the work day or work week are accompanied by an overall reduction in the standard of full-time paid work, the benefits to workers with family responsibilities are, at best, mixed.

Greater flexibility is needed to allow people to adjust their hours of work at particular times, for example, when family responsibilities are greatest. West Germany has experimented with a system of employment organization called flexiyear. Every employee contracts with an employer on

8

an annual basis to be employed for a certain amount of time, negotiating the hours per day, days per week, and months per year to be worked. Annual contracts are specified far enough in advance for employers to plan for appropriate deployment of their labour force. Employees have greater flexibility to modify their employment hours to accommodate other interests and to meet other demands on their time. All contracts of employment hours are equally protected in terms of benefits and security provisions. Wage rates are calculated on an annual scale, and wages for particular contracts are determined as a fraction of the annual rate, depending on the number of hours of employment in the contract. Employment per se is permanent and protected; in other words, there are separate agreements and procedures that apply to hiring for employment. The annual contracts involve negotiation only of hours. Although individual contracts may be for less or more than 30 hours per week, all employees are guaranteed a 30-hour-per-week minimum if they choose to work full-time hours.[18]

Reduced Hours and Part-time Work

One hundred years ago, full-time workers were employed for 9 to 10 hours a day, and the standard work week was approximately 65 hours.[19] By the end of World War II, the standard work week had been reduced by one-third, and 44 hours was the norm. Pressure from workers and their unions, technological innovations, improved methods of production, and the shift from agriculture to manufacturing were some of the factors behind this movement toward fewer working hours. Since the 1940s, hours of full-time work have continued to decline, but at a much slower pace. Provincial employment standards legislation sets a maximum on hours of work; the maximum varies from one jurisdiction to another, but nowhere is it less than 40 hours per week. In 1985, the average usual hours of full-time, paid work was 39 hours for women and 43 hours for men.[20]

Women's groups in several countries are arguing that a reduction in standard full-time hours, with or without reduced pay, is a necessary condition for more equitable sharing in parenting and household responsibilities. Trade unions are also either discussing or actively advocating a reduction in the standard work week, although their motives are primarily concerned with job creation and unemployment. In its submission to the Commission of Inquiry into Part-Time Work, the Canadian Labour Congress argued:

> the labour movement has long advocated a shorter week at no loss in pay for all workers, to equitably distribute any smaller amount of total work available as a result of productivity gains. We are not wedded to some magical virtue in the five-day, forty-hour week. We are open to at least discussing and negotiating flexible and innovative work arrangements...[21]

In Sweden, trade unions have proposed a 6-hour day and 30-hour week as the standard full-time employment, with the specific intention of achieving greater equality between women and men.

Even without the condition of no loss in pay, reducing the hours of full-time employment to 6 per day and 30 per week would significantly alter the potential time women and men who need full-time paycheques would have for a family life. With full-time working hours synchronized with the hours of full-time education for school children, problems of child care before and after school hours would be reduced.

A variant of the West German flexiyear concept could be established by improving the conditions associated with part-time work. In the general absence in Canada of either paid parental leave or planned flexibility of working hours, part-time work has become a major means of handling family responsibilities while remaining attached to the labour force. However, part-time work is not part of an organized scheme to facilitate the balance of life's activities. On the contrary, in most cases it is severely disadvantageous, providing limited work opportunities, low pay, few benefits, and no security. The Canadian Advisory Council on the Status of Women and other women's organizations are pressing for pay, benefits, and security for part-time work equal to those enjoyed by full-time workers. Such changes would have enormous benefits for women, since one-quarter of all women in the labour force are employed part-time. Also, it is only under these improved circumstances that part-time work might attract men and encourage them to share in raising their children.

Maternity and Parental Leave

Except for the Northwest Territories, all jurisdictions in Canada now have statutory provisions for maternity leave. These generally provide for 17 or 18 weeks of unpaid leave, although under the federal jurisdiction this has been increased to 24 weeks. Some even provide for mothers or fathers to take leave from employment on the birth of a child, and some also give adoptive parents the right to take leave when they adopt a child. Generally speaking, however, there is no statutory right to paid maternity or parental leave in Canada. Some unions have negotiated this right, through the collective bargaining process.

Since 1971, Canada has had a system of maternity benefits through the Unemployment Insurance (UI) program. However, the benefits are equivalent to only 60% of the worker's usual earnings, up to a maximum weekly limit. This limit is adjusted each year; in 1986, it was $297 a week. To be eligible for benefits, a woman must have worked and contributed to the UI program for a minimum of 20 weeks in the 52-week period before her claim. However employees who claim regular unemployment benefits need only work between 10 and 14 weeks to be eligible, depending on the unemployment rate in the region in which they live. The Parliamentary Sub-committee on Equality Rights has said that these different provisions are contrary to the equality clauses of the Canadian Charter of Rights and Freedoms.[22]

It must be noted that eligibility requirements laid down in federal and provincial labour codes and employment standards laws are often more strict than the UI regulations. In most cases, a woman must have worked for the same employer for at least a year to be eligible for maternity leave. It is thus possible to qualify for UI maternity benefits but to be unable to meet the statutory requirements to take maternity leave. Statutory leave provisions must be brought into line with programs providing benefits to parents, so that those who qualify to receive the benefits are also legally entitled to take the leave.

As with other benefits under the UI program, once a claimant has established her eligibility for maternity benefits, she does not receive any benefits for the first two weeks. (In Quebec these two weeks are covered by a flat-rate benefit of $240 from the provincial government. This provision was introduced in 1979 to compensate women for income lost during this period. This amount is not indexed and has not been increased since 1979.) After that, she may receive benefits for 15 weeks in total, but there are other restrictions. Maternity benefits extend over a 17-week period, which may be taken anywhere from 8 weeks before the expected birth of the child to 17 weeks after the actual date of birth. However, benefits from the UI program are not paid during a labour dispute. So a woman who becomes eligible to start receiving maternity benefits while her co-workers are on strike will not be able to get benefits until the strike is over, by which time she may find that the length of time left in her benefit period is considerably less than 17 weeks she had expected. As well, a woman who has made a claim for UI sickness benefits may find that she is not entitled to a full 15 weeks of maternity benefits when she becomes eligible, since there is a limit of 15 weeks in total on claims for maternity and sickness benefits combined.

Maternity benefits are available only to women, although UI benefits for adoptive parents, introduced at the beginning of 1984, may be claimed by either the mother or the father. Again, however, it must be noted that few jurisdictions provide a statutory right to leave on the adoption of a child.

Canada's maternity benefits program compares unfavourably with programs in most other countries of the industrialized world. A recent study noted that Canada ranked twenty-second out of 23 countries, mostly in eastern and western Europe, in terms of the level of benefits provided. Nineteen of the countries, including Italy, Ireland, Portugal, and Austria, have maternity benefits programs giving benefits equivalent to 80% to 100%

of the employee's usual earnings (often with a weekly maximum) for periods of between six weeks and nine months. Given that, under Canada's program, a claimant for benefits must forgo benefits completely for the first two weeks of her leave (except for the compensatory flat-rate benefit offered in Quebec), benefits received during the next 15 weeks actually represent only 53% of usual earnings when spread over the 17-week leave period. In Sweden, men and women have the right to be home for eight months with full pay following a child's birth.[23]

Some unions in Canada have negotiated collective agreements that provide for the employer to top up UI maternity benefits so that a worker on maternity leave will effectively receive full salary. A typical plan would provide for the employer to pay full salary during the initial two-week waiting period for UI maternity benefits and then to top up the next 15 weeks of benefits, from the 60% level provided by the UI program to an amount equivalent to 95% of the worker's usual earnings — the other 5% being accounted for by fringe benefits, which may continue during the leave period. Following this, there may be an additional three or four weeks during which the employer again pays full salary or 95% of salary. Provided that such a plan is registered by the employer as a Supplemental Unemployment Benefit (SUB) plan with the Canada Employment and Immigration Commission, the money received by employees does not count as earnings for the purposes of UI. Normally, any employment earnings have to be deducted from benefits paid by the UI program.

However, such agreements cover so few women that pressure is mounting for a national system of fully paid parental leave, so that all parents who combine paid work with family responsibilities would be able to take advantage of it. Such a program might be achieved by expanding the existing UI maternity benefits scheme and would involve increasing the level of benefits from the current 60% of insured earnings to 95%, to ensure that parents fulfilling childbearing and childrearing functions would not suffer a financial penalty, as they do now. Second, the length of the paid leave could be extended from the current 17 weeks to 26 weeks or longer. A 6-month leave was proposed initially, since this is the length of time many adoption agencies require an adopting parent to remain at home with a newly adopted child. Third, the paid leave would be made available to either parent, with parents able to choose which of them would take the paid leave. It has also been proposed that an improved paid parental leave plan be removed from the *Unemployment Insurance Act* and dealt with separately.

It has been estimated that a program that provides 26 weeks of fully paid leave would cost approximately $1.4 billion a year, if 65% of potential claimants actually received benefits. (The take-up rate for the existing maternity benefits program is thought to be only about 50%.) This estimate represents an additional cost, over and above that of the existing program, of about $978 million.[24] This could be funded through an increase in UI contributions amounting to only $1.24 a week at most for employees and a maximum of $1.75 a week for the employer contribution on behalf of each employee.[25] These calculations assume that the expanded program would be funded entirely by contributions from employers and employees (as maternity benefits now are funded) without any contribution from the federal government at all. Alternatively, under a program separate from UI, the federal government might be called upon to fund the additional benefits from general revenues.

The federal Task Force on Child Care (the Cooke Task Force, 1986), which also had a mandate to examine proposals for paid parental leave, recommended that the duration and level of birth and adoption benefits now available through the UI program be increased through a two-stage process. Within five years, the level of benefits should be increased to 75% of maximum insurable earnings and the period of leave extended to 20 weeks; within 10 years, the benefit rate should be increased to 95%, and the duration of the leave extended to 26 weeks.

The Task Force also recommended that birth and adoption benefits be made available to either parent in recognition of the equal partnership of parents in meeting family responsibilities.[26] While some members of the Task Force felt that a portion of the leave should be reserved for the mother only, to allow for her physical recuperation from the birth, others felt that parents should be given maximum freedom to allocate the benefit period between them, in whatever way suited their circumstances.

A system of paid parental leave for women and men — with no penalties incurred in terms of promotion, job training, income security, and other benefits — would greatly improve the conditions associated with combining parenting and paid work. Although alternatives for establishing a national system of paid parental leave in Canada have been researched, none has been implemented.

BARRIERS TO CHANGE

Improved hours of work will not be gained easily. Employers argue that shorter working hours are too costly, especially given the recent economic climate, and that such a change would reduce Canada's international competitiveness. These arguments have been used against every move toward improved working conditions. Yet earlier shifts to a shorter work week have not proved economically disastrous. No one anticipates an instant shift from 40 to 30 hours per week, with a consequent leap in labour costs. Rather, a gradual but definite move in that direction would spread cost increases over several years. Moreover, it can be argued that rapid introduction of new technology, resulting in increased productivity, will defray the costs of reduced working hours — and indeed, it is only fair that workers should

13

benefit in this way from the technological revolution now under way.

The push to reduce hours of work is not confined to Canada but is actually more advanced in several European countries; concern about our international competitive position is thus questionable. There are also many countries, particularly in the Third World, where workers are paid less, receive fewer benefits, and work longer hours than workers in Canada. Their existence does not force us to accept lower standards in this country.

As in past struggles for reduced working hours, trade union action will be critical. Thus far, union consideration of the issue has been dominated by the question of unemployment and the need to create more jobs. This approach is certainly valid, but it may result in pressure for reduced work time that would not benefit parents, and particularly women, in relation to family responsibilities. In 1984, the Canadian Labour Congress committed itself to work toward "shorter working time, with no loss of pay, including reduced work hours, paid educational leave, job retraining, earlier retirement and better pensions, and a ban on overtime." If early retirement and a ban on overtime become the only priorities, more jobs may be created, but little will have been gained in alleviating the problems experienced by women attempting to balance working for pay with raising children.

When it comes to employment standards, government action tends to follow other initiatives rather than lead the way. Women employed full-time work an average of 39 hours per week and men work 43, yet 6 of Canada's 13 jurisdictions still have a legislated maximum of 44 hours, and 2 are still at 48 hours per week. No jurisdiction has a legislated maximum of less than 40 hours per week. Nor has there been consideration given to reducing the legislated hours of work, although pressure is building for such action.

Reducing the hours of full-time work would not, of course, guarantee equitable sharing of childrearing and household maintenance between women and men. Husbands on flextime schedules do not help more with housework, although married women and single mothers on flextime spend up to two hours more per week on housework than those working standard hours. When wives are employed full-time, their husbands do not significantly increase their share of domestic work. Hours gained by men from a shorter paid work week will not necessarily be devoted to domestic labour. However, the shorter work week would establish the material conditions within which this sharing could be realistically negotiated. It would, in the meantime, certainly decrease the pressure and stress experienced by mothers in the paid labour force.

14

CONCLUSION

Since the 1950s, the standard hours of full-time work have remained stable while thousands of married women have joined the labour force. As a result, the hours of paid work put in by family members, both men and women, have increased over the last 35 years. The result is added pressure to meet the demands of paid work and family responsibilities. To date, the necessary adjustments have been made within families, especially by women changing their work patterns over time, often to their personal and financial detriment. We must consider, instead, how the organization of paid work can be adapted to the realities of today's families.

NOTES

1. Andrew S. Harvey, David H. Elliott and W. Stephen Macdonald, *The Work of Canadians: Explorations in Time Use*, vol. 3 (Ottawa: Employment and Immigration Canada, 1983), tables 7 and 9, pp. 33, 35.

2. *Ibid.*

3. Canada, Statistics Canada, *The Labour Force* (Ottawa: Supply and Services Canada, 1985), catalogue no. 71-001, table 61A.

4. William Michelson, *From Sun to Sun: Daily Obligations and Community Structure in the Lives of Employed Women and Their Families* (Towata, New Jersey: Rowan and Allanheld, 1985), pp. 75-85.

5. *Ibid.*

6. Canada, Statistics Canada, *The Labour Force*, table 80.

7. Julie White, *Women and Part-Time Work*, Canadian Advisory Council on the Status of Women (Ottawa: Supply and Services Canada, 1983).

8. Canada, Statistics Canada, *The Labour Force*, table 80.

9. Susan Clark and Andrew S. Harvey, "The Sexual Division of Labour: The Use of Time", *Atlantis*, vol. 2, no. 1 (Fall 1976), table 5, p. 61.

10. Canada, Statistics Canada, *The Labour Force*, table 76.

11. Canada, Statistics Canada, special tabulation from the Labour Force Survey Division (Ottawa: 1984).

12. William Michelson, *From Sun to Sun*, p. 93.

13. E. Stoper, "Alternative Work Patterns and the Double Life", in *Women, Power and Policy*, ed. E. Boneparth (Toronto: Pergamon Press, 1982).

14. *Ibid.*, p. 92.

15. "Four-Day Work Week Gaining Support", *The Citizen* [Ottawa], August 14, 1986, p. 11.

16. Halcyone H. Bohen and Anamaria Viveros-Long, *Balancing Jobs and Family Life: Do Flexible Work Schedules Help?* (Philadelphia: Temple University Press, 1981).

17. *Ibid.*, p. 147.

18. Ben Malkin, "The Flexible Future", *Worklife*, vol. 2, no. 3 (1982), pp. 5-6; "Time: Flexiyears", *Worklife*, vol. 3 (1983), p. 12.

19. Canada, Statistics Canada, *Workers with Long Hours*, Special Labour Force Studies Series A, no. 9 (Ottawa: Supply and Services Canada, 1972), catalogue no. 71-518, table 18, p. 40.

20. Canada, Statistics Canada, *The Labour Force*, table 79.

21. Canadian Labour Congress, "A Submission to the Commission of Inquiry into Part-Time Work" (Ottawa, September 3, 1982), p. 12.

22. Canada, House of Commons, Parliamentary Sub-committee on Equality Rights, *Equality for All* (Ottawa: Supply and Services Canada, 1985), p. 14.

23. Berit Rollen, "Gently Towards Equality", *Working Life in Sweden*, no. 5 (Stockholm: Swedish Information Service, 1978).

24. Monica Townson, "Paid Parental Leave Policies: An International Comparison, with Options for Canada", in *Child Care: The Employer's Role*, Background paper prepared for *Report of the Task Force on Child Care*, Series 4 (Ottawa: Status of Women Canada, 1985), p. 9.

25. Status of Women Canada, *Report of the Task Force on Child Care* (Ottawa: 1986), pp. 314-316.

26. Monica Townson, "Paid Parental Leave Policies", p. 46.

CHAPTER TWO

MARRIAGE AND MONEY[1]

Millions of women who would normally insist on knowing their rights before borrowing as little as $100 happily enter into the most important financial contract of their lives — marriage — without having the least idea of what it is all about. For the few marriages where the spouses always agree on everything, this does not make any difference. However, for the women whose unions are less than perfect, and most of all for the 40% or so whose marriages end in divorce, the consequences can be devastating.

The laws regulating matrimonial property come under the jurisdiction of each province and territory. The result is that a wife's right to family income and assets, for example, can vary in crucial ways, depending on whether she lives in Newfoundland, Quebec, Saskatchewan, or British Columbia. In addition, spouses can change the rules that would normally apply to them by entering into individualized marriage contracts. Few couples take this extra step, except in the province of Quebec, where, for historical reasons, a large proportion of husbands and wives opt out of the standard regime by signing such contracts.

As if all these varying legislative requirements were not complicated enough, some aspects of family law are not regulated by the provinces and territories, but come under the jurisdiction of the federal government. The main one is divorce; the federal *Divorce Act* determines under what conditions a divorce can take place and what support or maintenance payments — if any — are to be made when it happens. This does not include division between spouses of the property they own at the time their marriage is dissolved, because that continues to be regulated by provincial and territorial law.

In the last 20 years, almost all of these laws have been completely transformed to modernize them and improve the status of women. The *Divorce Act* of 1968 introduced no-fault grounds for divorce, such as separation for a few years. In the infamous *Murdoch* case of 1974, it was held that an Alberta ranch wife who worked alongside her husband for 25 years was entitled to none of the assets they had accumulated under his name during the marriage because she had acted like "any ranch wife".[2] Following this case, all provinces changed their laws to correct such injustices and give more property rights to divorcing women.

However, in spite of these improvements, women are still not treated as equal partners within marriage. Wives who have no earnings of their own, or whose incomes are much lower than those of their husbands, are particularly vulnerable. Too many find out that the words "I endow thee with all my worldly goods" have no legal significance in Canada. As a result, young women who expect their future husbands to support them for life are running a grave risk of ending up alone and in poverty. The National Council of Welfare estimated that although about 90% of women marry, three-quarters of them will eventually be forced to look after their own financial needs and those of their families.[3]

To dispel unrealistic expectations about marriage, it is important to know what being married really means in Canada today. The three main aspects to be considered are the financial consequences of marriage in the following situations: while the spouses are living together, after they divorce, and following the husband's death.

FINANCES DURING THE MARRIAGE

As no extensive survey of the financial dealings of Canadian spouses has ever been conducted, there is no means of knowing how couples actually share their money and make economic decisions. The few studies — all from the United States — that looked at power relationships within the family concluded that "marital power is a function of income to a large extent."[4] The higher a spouse's income and occupational status, the greater his or her weight in making important decisions.

The other factor affecting each spouse's economic position is the legal rights that a wife or husband can claim in relation to the couple's belongings and the earnings that come into the family. These rights fall under two main headings: rights of ownership and management, and rights to be supported by the other spouse.

The general rule relating to ownership and management of the couple's earnings and assets during the marriage is that unless they have made other arrangements through a marriage contract, each spouse is entitled to do what he or she wants with the property he or she personally acquires. As a result, wives and husbands are almost completely free to save or squander their own earnings, investments, inheritances or other money as they wish. Conversely, neither has any rights over the money and property acquired by the other spouse.

There are two main exceptions to this general rule. The first, which is intended to protect the spouses' future rights, prevents husbands and wives from disposing of their property in a way that would render meaningless the other spouse's right to a share of it upon divorce or death. One example is in the Quebec Civil Code, which prevents a husband or wife married under the basic partnership of acquests regime (meaning they did not have a marriage contract) from giving away his or her shareable assets,

20

except for modest sums and customary presents, without the consent of the other spouse. The closest counterpart in the other provinces is a universal clause allowing a spouse to apply to the courts to restrain the squandering of property or its transfer for less than its value in ways that would defeat a claim of the other spouse.

The second type of exception was enacted to protect the matrimonial home. In all provinces except Quebec and British Columbia, the spouse who owns a matrimonial home cannot sell it, mortgage it, rent it, or otherwise dispose of it without the written consent of the other spouse or a judge's order dispensing with it. This right is automatic, and no prior registration is required. In Quebec and British Columbia, the non-owner spouse must register her or his right beforehand, which makes the provision quite useless in practice.

The second category of rights is those related to support. According to the legal obligation of support, spouses must provide each other with at least minimal food, housing, and clothing in case of need. This does not mean that a full-time homemaker, for instance, is entitled to cash money of her own, because a husband who pays for the groceries, rent, and clothing directly is in full compliance with the law. The only exception is in Manitoba, whose law specifies that a non-earning spouse has a right to "periodic reasonable amounts" for personal expenses and can also demand to be kept informed of the state of the family's finances.[5]

Practically speaking, however, the right to support is not worth much, for the simple reason that wives who quarrel with their husbands over money do not take them to court while they are still living together. As for the historical right of wives to engage their husbands' credit to buy necessities for the family, it is also illusory, since tradespeople are very unlikely to extend credit to housewives without their husbands' signatures.

Thus, Canadian wives with no personal sources of income are far from enjoying equal rights to their families' money. All the main proposals for improving this situation involve some form of co-ownership and joint management of the income and assets that both spouses acquire through their own efforts during the marriage.

Until now, women's groups have been so busy working on trying to obtain a fairer share of the family's assets for divorcing wives that few have developed detailed positions on the financial relations of couples whose marriages are intact. The Canadian Advisory Council on the Status of Women believes that the relevant laws should reflect two principles in particular: the right of the partners during the marriage to an equal, continuing share of the security being built up for the future (for example, pensions, superannuation credits and tax-free savings); and the responsibility of the partners during the marriage to support one another with services and/or finances to reflect the concept of marriage as an interdependent partnership of shared responsibilities.[6]

One approach would be to adopt a system of community property with joint management by both spouses during the marriage. Under such a system — which already exists in seven U.S. states[7] — the spouses would be immediate co-owners and co-managers of almost everything either of them acquires while they are living together. Even more important in many cases, this system allows homemakers to borrow money on the basis of their husbands' earnings (without the husbands' signatures) and entitles these women to make wills leaving their share of the couple's property to whomever they want.

It may be a long time before such reforms are introduced in Canada, but this does not concern people who believe that the best possible matrimonial arrangement for any woman is an individually tailored marriage contract. The problem with this view is that although a marriage contract might be ideal for a woman who knows what she wants and is aware of her rights, it could be very dangerous for less well informed brides, who may end up with fewer rights than they would have had under the standard law.

MONEY AFTER LOVE HAS GONE

Almost 40% of new marriages end in divorce. Divorce has ceased to be an exceptional situation and is on its way to becoming an established institution. Commentators have recently tended to play down its negative aspects, and to hail it instead as "a signal of healthy adaptability, with the emergence of new types of families and new social groupings that may be more attuned to people's real needs."[8] This attitude was epitomized in a 1983 *Maclean's* article, where a divorcée whose 13-year marriage had recently ended was quoted as saying, "My life has steadily improved, and right now I would say it's pretty well perfect."[9]

In reality, typical divorcées are emphatically not having a wonderful time. According to Statistics Canada, 40% of them find themselves alone with young children to bring up; another 10% are over 50 years old at the time of their divorce.[10] While it is true that three-quarters of divorced women remarry (compared with 83% of divorced men), it would be a grave error to conclude that everything works out for the best in most cases. On the contrary, studies show that many women who remarry, particularly low-income women with young children, do so less by choice than because of absolute economic necessity.[11] Self-sufficient childless women are least likely to take a new spouse.

To understand what most divorcing women live through, let us follow the hypothetical case of Mary Ann S., an Ontario woman from a respectable working-class background. Her father is a bus driver and her mother a homemaker. When Mary Ann got pregnant at the age of 18, in her

22

last year of high school, she and her boyfriend, Jim, decided to get married. Five years later, Jim told Mary Ann, who had been keeping house and raising their two children in a home in the suburbs, that he intended to leave her to go and live with another woman. As their marriage had not been a happy one for some time, she decided to give up on the relationship and get a divorce.

Stage 1 — Legal Aid

Because Mary Ann had no money of her own, getting a lawyer meant applying for legal aid, a provincial government program that provides free legal services to those who cannot afford them. Although going to the legal aid office was not exactly painful, it was nevertheless somewhat unpleasant. Why should Mary Ann have to wait in line, fill out innumerable forms, and answer indiscreet questions when all her husband had to do was pick up the phone and hire himself a lawyer? It seemed unfair — and it was.

Stage 2 — Getting Support and a Share of the Property

The first thing Mary Ann's lawyer did was apply for interim alimony (for Mary Ann) and maintenance (for the children) to provide for their needs in the interval between the original divorce petition and the trial. Mary Ann had prepared a very strict budget showing that she could not possibly stay in the house and make ends meet with less than $1,250 a month. Her husband, who was a mechanic earning $1,500 net a month, also produced a budget showing that he needed $1,000 a month to be able to live at a minimal level, pay for his car, and continue to make deposits on an old debt for items he had bought many years before. Jim's statement also showed that his assets consisted of his car (worth $5,000), a $1,000 deposit in a registered retirement savings plan, and the unmortgaged part of the house ($10,000).

Saying that no useful purpose would be served by bankrupting Jim, the judge ordered him to continue to make the mortgage payments on the house ($400 a month) until the trial and to pay an additional $250 a month to Mary Ann for the rest of the family's needs. Remarking to Mary Ann that she was young and healthy, he suggested she try to find a job. In the few months before the trial, Mary Ann thought she would go out of her mind. She tried to look for jobs, but couldn't do it without a baby-sitter, and she had no money to pay one. She got by only because her parents gave her some food when she ran out.

At the trial, her lawyer advised her to accept the following offer from her husband: a lump-sum settlement equal to two-thirds of the net proceeds of selling the house, along with $650 in monthly support payments, to be reduced to $500 two years later when Mary Ann would presumably be able to assume her own maintenance. Mary Ann agreed.

How does Mary Ann's case compare with typical Canadian divorces? We will find out by examining, first, division of property between the spouses, and second, eligibility for support and determination of its amount.

■ Division of property

The total value of the property involved in Mary Ann's case amounted to $16,000, which is typical of couples who divorce after five years of marriage. A recent U.S. survey concluded that "The first and perhaps most important fact...about marital property is that many divorcing couples have little or no property to divide... Because most divorcing couples are relatively young and in the lower-income groups, this should not be surprising."[12]

In the relatively few cases where Canadian spouses have assets of some substance, their division is regulated by provincial matrimonial property laws. The simplest are those applying to spouses married under the partnership of acquests regime in the province of Quebec. It provides that everything the spouses owned before the marriage, or acquired at any time by way of gift or inheritance, as well as a few other clearly specified items, remain separate property that is never shared between them at any time. Everything else is shared equally between husbands and wives at the time of their divorce.

The laws of the other provinces differ in varying degrees, but common elements stand out:

■ a basic principle of equal sharing of a given category of assets, the definition of which varies from province to province;

■ a provision that contributions through money or work to a business or farm entitle a spouse to a share of that property; and

■ an overriding judicial discretion enabling judges to vary the equal shares established under the basic sharing principle mentioned above, or to include in them other categories of assets that are not subject to the equal sharing presumption.

24

Table 2.1   Typical Distribution of Assets on Divorce in Long-term Marriages

	Home and Contents, Car and Cottage	Private Pension Rights	RRSPs	Businesses and Farms
British Columbia	Shared equally	Shared equally	Shared equally	Shared equally if the wife worked both at home and outside; homemakers get 1/4 to 1/3.
Alberta	Shared equally	Shared equally	Shared equally	Same as B.C.
Saskatchewan	Shared equally	Shared equally	Shared equally	Shared equally
Manitoba	Shared equally	Shared equally	Shared equally	Shared equally
Ontario	Shared equally	Shared equally	Shared equally	Shared equally
Quebec (partnership of acquests)	Shared equally	Not shared	Shared equally	Shared equally
New Brunswick	Shared equally	Sometimes shared equally	Shared equally	Sharing varies depending on assessment of each spouse's contribution.
Nova Scotia	Shared equally	Shared equally	Sometimes shared equally	Same as N.B.
Prince Edward Island	Shared equally	Not shared	Sometimes shared equally	Shared equally if wife worked both at home and outside; housewives get little or none.
Newfoundland	Shared equally	Shared equally	Shared equally	Same as New Brunswick and Nova Scotia

Note: Except in Quebec, the sharing described here is neither automatic nor guaranteed.

Source: *Canadian Family Law Guide*, vol. 1 (Don Mills: CCH Canadian); and A. Bisset-Johnson and W.H. Holland, *Matrimonial Property Law in Canada* (Agincourt, Ont.: Burroughs).

The result of this overriding discretion, which is much broader in some provinces than in others (it is practically unlimited in Alberta, but was severely cut back in Saskatchewan by a decision of the Supreme Court of Canada[13]), is that the outcome of any individual case is quite unpredictable. Inasmuch as any pattern can be discerned in the cases reported so far, typical judgements are shown in Table 2.1.

According to the table, Saskatchewan, Manitoba, and Ontario have the most egalitarian family property laws in Canada, and Prince Edward Island has the least. The former three provinces are the only ones that give wives an equal right to all the assets acquired through the spouses' efforts during their life together. Quebec still fails to divide pension rights, which have now become, along with the matrimonial home, the most important asset of divorcing couples. The rest of the provinces do not entitle ex-wives to an equal share of the businesses and farms acquired in their husbands' names during the marriage, but rely instead on judicial discretion to determine the extent of each spouse's contribution. This lets judges apply their personal values to each case, with predictably uneven and inequitable results.

■   Eligibility for support and determination of its amount

Mary Ann's support payments out of her ex-husband's salary of $1,500 a month amounted to $650 a month for two years and $500 after that until the children were grown. This meant that he got to keep $850 for himself, or 57%, which seems quite unfair, since he had only himself to support, while Mary Ann had to support three people.

This type of support is not typical: Mary Ann's award was considerably higher than the average. A Statistics Canada study found that the average amount of support ordered in this country is about 20% of the husband's net income, while the median amount is closer to 17%.[14] A recent major survey of support payments in Alberta found that only 5% of ex-wives received periodic awards for themselves. Even when dependent children were involved, only 18% of ex-wives were granted such awards.[15]

Child support is much more common. In the Alberta cases involving dependent children, 65% of the custodial parents were awarded periodic amounts for the children. The amounts were usually much less generous than Mary Ann's award, with nearly half the Alberta awards being between $101 and $200 per child per month. The next largest category was between $51 and $100 a month.

The depressing implication of these figures is that husbands are much better off after a divorce than are their former wives and children.

26

When the post-divorce incomes of the spouses (less support) are divided by the number of people in their new households, the gap between former and present standards of living of ex-wives and ex-husbands becomes a gulf. This is the result of the husband keeping most of the family's money, while the wife takes charge of all its dependants.

The inevitable outcome is that, while the standard of living of wives and children collapses upon marriage breakdown, that of husbands rises to the point where they have almost twice as much disposable income as they had before their families split up. This has led some people to say that it is not feminism, or the disappearance of old family values, that is causing the dissolution of so many marriages today, but the simple fact that the present system, with its easy divorces and very low support awards, is providing large numbers of men with a strong financial incentive to abandon their wives and children.[16]

Also obvious from the figures on support awards is the weakness of the frequently heard argument that many divorced men are being soaked by cruel ex-wives who extort from them exorbitant maintenance payments. The truth, as found by the Manitoba Law Reform Commission, is that

> Sometimes the payment of child support is assessed and awarded at unrealistically low amounts. People, including the father who is paying court-awarded child maintenance, complained to us that in some areas of the province child maintenance is being fixed by the court as low as $25 per month.[17]

Another common myth about maintenance payments is that it is pointless to try to collect them because most ex-husbands have no money. In fact, Canadian as well U.S. surveys have repeatedly confirmed that more than 80% of support defaulters are able to pay.[18] This does not mean that most ex-husbands are well-off, but that their capacity to pay was already taken into account — and usually underestimated — when the amount of their support order was determined by the court.

Compounding these problems is the fact that no two judges seem to agree on the criteria that should be used to calculate the amount of support payments. This led expert Judith Cassetty of the University of Texas to conclude that

> there are no readily discernible implicit or explicit standards for support payments... There is enormous variance between and within jurisdictions in both orders for support and payment performance...[19]

To improve the situation, it has been proposed that objective standards be developed for calculating support amounts. If this were done, and the whole matter handled by computers, some experts say, a great deal of court time would be saved that could be spent more profitably on matters in which judges are more competent.[20]

Returning to the point raised earlier concerning the small proportion of ex-wives who are awarded support payments for themselves, the issue is the criteria judges use in deciding who is eligible for support and who is not. In the 1970s and early 1980s, judges tended increasingly to adopt the so-called clean break approach, under which ex-wives who were not financially independent were given one to three years within which to become self-supporting, no matter how long they had been out of the labour force or how obsolete their skills. This ruthless approach was checked in November 1983 by the Supreme Court of Canada decision in the case of *Messier* v. *Delage*, in which it was held that an ex-wife should continue to be eligible for alimony payments until she had actually acquired independent means of support.[21]

The next unfortunate development was adoption of a new *Divorce Act*, which had the effect of reversing the *Messier* v. *Delage* decision. The new law, which came into force on June 2, 1986, makes it clear that short-term maintenance orders are valid and specifies further that such orders cannot be varied or extended unless the ex-wife can prove that there has been a change in her situation. Women's groups strongly objected to this, pointing out that "wives who cannot find a job in the prescribed period will find themselves in a classic catch-22 situation, since their problem is precisely that no change has occurred in their position."[22] Instead, feminists wanted the law to include support criteria that would

■ recognize that thousands of middle-aged housewives who are now divorcing will never become self-sufficient and should therefore be entitled to long-term support at reasonable levels;

■ provide for retraining of ex-wives who are in a position to benefit from it, by subsidizing their education up to and including post-graduate studies, thereby discouraging short-term training, which streams women into low-income female employment ghettos; and

■ respect a parent's choice to stay home with her/his young children, if the other parent can afford it and if this is what the couple had originally planned.

Despite pressures from women, however, these criteria were not included in the new legislation.

Stage 3 — Collection and Default

After the divorce, Mary Ann's life became quite austere. She scrubbed her small apartment, laundered, cooked, and watched television. Her parents bought her a portable typewriter and a manual on typing. Meanwhile, Jim and his new companion, who was a sales clerk, bought a small house outside town. His contacts with the children gradually became less frequent, and when the improvements he was making to his new home cost more than anticipated, he started to forget to send his maintenance payments.

Thanks to Ontario's new system of automatic enforcement of maintenance orders, which threatened to seize Jim's salary if he did not comply rapidly, the problem was soon corrected. Mary Ann was fortunate by comparison with divorced women from most other provinces, who must start collection procedures anew, month after month and at considerable financial and emotional cost.

Only Manitoba, Ontario, Saskatchewan, and Alberta have fully automatic systems for collecting maintenance payments, using computerized systems that register all maintenance orders. They routinely issue everlasting garnishee orders forcing employers to deduct support payments continually from salaries and send them to the courts or the ex-spouses. Quebec also has a non-automatic system, under which ex-spouses who are not receiving their payments can apply to a special collection service that tracks down defaulters and seizes their wages for as long as a year.

Before these new systems were introduced, default was so widespread that it inspired the Law Reform Commission of Canada to write the following much-quoted passage:

> Something is profoundly wrong with a body of law and practice that fails to attain its objects more often than it succeeds. Failure is the universal characteristic of the traditional system for enforcing maintenance orders in Canada...
>
> The burden of this social evil is and always has been carried by women, most of whom are found in the least economically influential strata in Canada...[23]

The main ways of solving the problem of enforcing support orders include the following:

- setting up **self-starting** systems for collecting maintenance that are not based on complaints filed by ex-wives;

- using **continuing wage garnishment** to seize payments in the hands of the defaulters' employers as soon as they become due;

29

- making **all sources of income and types of properties** subject to seizure for payment of maintenance debts, including pensions, unemployment benefits, and tax refunds;

- enforcing **separation agreements** in the same manner as enforcement of court-ordered awards;

- obliging all governments, agencies, and individuals to divulge all the **information** they have on the whereabouts and employment situation of people who owe support;

- keeping **imprisonment** as a last resort, and using it firmly when nothing else will do; and

- committing of the **necessary resources**, by all levels of government, to ensure that the collection systems have the computer equipment and staff they need to work efficiently.

The next official news Mary Ann received from her ex-husband was through a notice informing her that he had applied to the court to have his maintenance payments reduced because his expenses had risen. The reason for the increase in his costs was that he had married his live-in companion, who had left her job following the birth of their child. Mary Ann was outraged, but there was little she could do. When the case got to court, her support was cut from $500 a month (the first two years having expired) to $250. She had no other option but to apply for welfare.

Stage 4 — Interprovincial Collection and Welfare

Two years later, Jim and his new family moved to Alberta, and he decided to stop making payments to his first family. This forced Mary Ann to become involved in the question of interprovincial enforcement of maintenance orders; what she found was that the present system is a mess.

The first problem is that no interprovincial tracing system exists to find the whereabouts of defaulting spouses/fathers. The second is that even if they are found, the support order cannot be enforced in the other province without being recognized there first, a process that can be very complicated in some cases, and almost always requires hiring and paying an out-of-province lawyer. Even if all the steps are completed successfully, enforcement of the order will be only as good as the enforcement of local orders, which is poor in most provinces.

The best means of correcting these problems would involve the following steps:

- Giving the courts or provincial collection agencies access to government data banks to locate absconding spouses/fathers. Procedures to start doing this at the federal level are under way, with the necessary legislation having been approved to give access to the information contained in the Canada Pension Plan and Social Insurance Register files starting in 1987.

- Empowering divorce courts to issue continuing garnishment orders that would not need to be registered anew for other provinces but would have effect throughout Canada.

- Collecting maintenance payments through the mechanisms of the Department of National Revenue. This would not require many additional resources, since that department is already in constant communication with all employers for the purpose of collecting income taxes.

- Establishing a Swedish-style government program that would make advance payments to the families of maintenance defaulters. The families would thus have a regular and secure source of income, and the government would reimburse itself by collecting the amounts due from delinquent fathers and ex-husbands.

Many months and a great deal of trouble later, Mary Ann succeeded in tracking down Jim in Alberta and getting him to resume his payments. This came at a good time, because Mary Ann had just gotten off welfare to start her very first paid job as a receptionist, thus becoming self-supporting for the first time in her life.

LOVE, MARRIAGE AND DEATH

The story of Mary Ann thus ended reasonably well: the worriers in her family were then free to transfer their concern to Mary Ann's mother, Betty, who was also having spousal money problems of her own.

Betty's marriage had not been a very happy one, but she and her husband had nevertheless reached a peaceful understanding long ago. They both had their own interests and occupations, and their contacts with each other were minimal. If it ever occurred to Betty to wonder what would happen when her husband died, she would probably have thought that things would continue as before. When he did die, however, Betty was shocked to find that he had left a will giving all his savings to the children and their home to a gardening society. Betty was left at 55 years of age with nothing but the meagre maximum widow's pension of $273 a month from the Canada Pension Plan.

Her lawyer informed her that she was very fortunate, because Ontario's family law — unlike that of Prince Edward Island, Alberta, British

Columbia, or the two territories — had just been changed to give widows the same right to a share of the couple's property as it gives to divorcing wives. If her husband had died a couple of years earlier, he said, her only recourse would have been to apply to the courts to ask that the will be set aside to give her enough money to support herself at a minimal level.

This would have been a humiliating process, involving an examination of her lifestyle and resources. Under the new law, however, Betty was entitled to claim half the value of all the assets and properties she and her husband had accumulated during their marriage. This did not make her rich, but it allowed her to maintain a decent standard of living.

Because of the unfortunate situations facing wives in provinces that do not provide for the sharing of family assets on death, and because of the appalling poverty of most widowed elderly Canadian women, it has been recommended that:

- all family laws entitle widows to property rights at least as generous as those of divorced spouses;

- dependent ex-spouses be able to claim support from the estate after the death of the other spouse; and

- pension laws be improved to guarantee an adequate minimal income to everyone over the age of 60; to expand the Canada/Quebec Pension Plan for all earners, split the pension between spouses, and extend coverage to homemakers; and to overhaul employer-sponsored pension plans, especially with regard to inflation protection and benefits for surviving spouses.

CONCLUSION

Marriage and the family are here to stay, but they are no longer the only focus of women's lives. Increasing pressure is also being brought to bear on these institutions by independent young women who refuse to accept their restrictions. Faced with customs that make them almost solely responsible for bringing up the children and laws that deny them equal control over the couple's finances, these young women are reacting by being less inclined to marry,[24] by marrying at a later age[25] and, even more important, by having much smaller families than their mothers did.[26]

A transformation of the family is also being caused by the tremendously increased frequency of marital breakdown and the ease of divorce. Forty per cent of today's marriages are expected to end in divorce, and when they do, our present laws ensure that the advantages and disadvantages flowing from the marriage will be unevenly distributed between the spouses. While divorce usually means financial disaster for women, it almost invariably entails a substantial increase in the standard of living of men. As a result, the present system encourages low-income husbands to abandon their families.

The four most important steps that our society must take to improve this situation are

- demystifying the institution of marriage so that young people will know all its risks as well as its joys;

- a radical review of our family laws to fully recognize women's work in the family and make them equal partners in marriage;

- eliminating all barriers to the full integration of women in all aspects of society;

- adopting positive steps to actively encourage integration of women in the paid labour force, including increased access to better-paying jobs and good-quality, affordable child care services.

NOTES

1. This chapter is a condensed and updated version of Louise Dulude, *Love, Marriage and Money: An Analysis of Financial Relations Between the Spouses* (Ottawa: Canadian Advisory Council on the Status of Women, 1984).

2. *Murdoch* v. *Murdoch* (1974), 13 R.F.L. 185.

3. National Council of Welfare, *Women and Poverty* (Ottawa: 1979), pp. 25-26.

4. Dair L. Gillespie, "Who Has the Power? The Marital Struggle", *Journal of Marriage and the Family*, vol. 33, no. 3 (1971), p. 451.

5. Manitoba, *Family Maintenance Act*, s. 3 and s. 6.

6. Canadian Advisory Council on the Status of Women, *Recommendations* (Ottawa: 1986), C1.1.

7. Arizona, California, Idaho, Nevada, New Mexico, Washington, and Louisiana.

8. Angela Ferrante, "Coming to Terms with Divorce", *Maclean's* (March 21, 1983), p. 39.

9. *Ibid.*, p. 40.

10. D.C. McKie, B. Prentice and P. Reed, *Divorce, Law and the Family in Canada*, Statistics Canada (Ottawa: Supply and Services Canada, 1983), pp. 145, 214; Canada, Statistics Canada, *Vital Statistics*, Volume II, *Marriages and Divorces, 1981* (Ottawa: Supply and Services Canada, 1983), catalogue no. 84-205, p. 22.

11. Helen P. Koo and C.M. Suchindran, "Effects of Children on Women's Remarriage Prospects", *Journal of Family Issues*, vol. 1, no. 4 (1980), p. 497.

12. Lenore J. Weitzman, "The Economics of Divorce: Social and Economic Consequences of Property, Alimony and Child Support Awards", in *International Invitational Conference on Matrimonial and Child Support — Conference Materials*, May 27-30, 1981 (Edmonton: Institute of Law Research and Reform, 1982), p. 53.

13. *Farr* v. *Farr*, Supreme Court of Canada, May 3, 1984.

14. B. Prentice, C. McKie and P. Reed, *Divorce And Custody in Ontario: An Analysis of a Sample of Files for 1975 from the Office of the Official Guardian of Ontario*, Statistics Canada, Justice Statistics Division, Research Study no. 7 (Ottawa: Supply and Services Canada, 1979), p. 32.

15. Canadian Institute for Research, *Matrimonial Support Failures: Reasons, Profiles and Perceptions of Individuals Involved*, Volume II, prepared for the Institute of Law Research and Reform (Edmonton: Institute of Law Research and Reform, 1981), pp. 49-52.

16. Barbara Ehrenreich, "The 'Playboy' Man and the American Family", *Ms* (June 1983), p. 14.

17. Manitoba Law Reform Commission, *Report on Family Law*, Part 1, *The Support Obligation*, Report no. 23 (Winnipeg, 1976), p. 10.

18. Judith Cassetty, *Child Support and Public Policy: Securing Support from Absent Parents* (Lexington: D.C. Heath, 1978), pp. 63-83; Canadian Institute for Research, *Matrimonial Support Failures*, vol. 1, p. 22.

19. Judith Cassetty, "Matrimonial Support Failures: Reasons, Profiles and Perceptions of Individuals Involved: A Commentary", in *International Invitational Conference on Matrimonial and Child Support*, pp. 30-31.

20. Kenneth R. White and R. Thomas Stone, "A Study of Alimony and Child Support Findings with Some Recommendations", *Family Law Quarterly*, vol. 10, no. 1 (1976), p. 83.

21. *Messier* v. *Delage*, Supreme Court of Canada, November 3, 1983, no. 16806.

22. National Action Committee on the Status of Women and National Association of Women and the Law, "Joint Press Release of the National Action Committee on the Status of Women and of the National Association of Women and the Law on the Minister of Justice's New Proposals on Divorce", October 15, 1985.

23. Edward Ryan, *Family Law — Enforcement of Maintenance Orders*, Information Canada (Ottawa: Supply and Services Canada, 1976), p. 47.

24. Marriage rate calculated from Canada, Statistics Canada, *Vital Statistics*, Volume II.

25. Ages at marriage calculated from the same source as in note 24.

26. Birth rates from Canada, Statistics Canada, *Vital Statistics*, Volume I, *Births and Deaths, 1981* (Ottawa: Supply and Services Canada, 1983), catalogue no. 84-204.

CHAPTER THREE

NO VACANCIES! WOMEN AND UNEMPLOYMENT

The Women's Employment Centre, situated in a Toronto shopping mall, is one of a handful of Canada Employment Centres (CECs) in Canada devoted exclusively to counselling and employment services for women.[1] The brightly lit centre, spotted with cheerful posters of women doing non-traditional work, is in the heart of what is known locally as the Jane-Finch corridor — a neighbourhood characterized by high-rises, low-rental housing, and some of the serious social problems that come with high unemployment. The centre's plate glass doors, windows, and posters attract passers-by as well as women clients referred from CECs across the city.

Joanne, a graduate student in adult education, came to the Jane-Finch Women's Employment Centre in 1982 as part of her professional training in employment and career counselling. She agreed to take on a series of creative job search strategy groups, giving unemployed women a two-day crash course in contacting employers, putting together a résumé, and looking for a job. But this was 1982 — the height of the recession — and she quickly found that her main preoccupation was simply "coping with the load".

Feelings of discouragement and helplessness ran deep in each job search group. Although Joanne had some general familiarity with labour market issues, her understanding "couldn't have prepared [her] for the sheer volume and diversity of clients pouring in through the door that September." Her reflections on her time at Jane-Finch express the specific conflicts and tensions experienced by employment counsellors meeting the demands of front-line employment counselling in a shrinking job market:

> The women I met there could not be classified into neat pigeonholes. I had women with Master's degrees who were willing to take on clerical work. There were numerous laid-off retail workers — usually women who worked in clothing stores. These people had worked steadily for ten, fifteen years in one place and then were suddenly told: no job. There were experienced secretaries who had been looking for six months, who typed at the appropriate speed employers were supposed to be looking for, but still no jobs. There were the immigrant women, laid off their minimum wage jobs that did not support them adequately in the

first place. Sometimes these women also had laid-off husbands. I realized very quickly that merely teaching the knowledge I had to impart on being clever and creative about job hunting methods would simply not produce the jobs for these women. There were far too many — many with the same kind of skills and often looking for more sales or clerical. Most of these women could not afford the luxury of long-term career planning, or retraining on the pittance available. They were stuck, and so was I, in that situation.

Joanne's concerns about the women she counselled in 1982 raise questions about how women are affected by unemployment. Women suffer the consequences of unemployment directly when they lose their jobs, but there are also less direct effects. Women workers are underemployed when they have to accept part-time work because no full-time jobs are available — and more and more women are having to do this. Part-time work can be desirable for women who want to combine paid employment with family responsibilities. Often, however, women (and their families) need the income that only a full-time job can supply; and the percentage of women who work part-time when they would prefer full-time employment is increasing. Women also account for an increasing percentage of the **hidden unemployed** — those workers who leave the labour force in despair of ever finding work.

Most women who work for pay outside the home also work without pay inside their homes. When paid employment disappears, unpaid homemaking work is always there and waiting. Indeed, there is evidence that during hard economic times, the work of the homemaker becomes more onerous. As Pat Armstrong points out in a recent book on women's employment,

> economic crises are not restricted to the formal economy because households and the formal economy overlap. Workers are also consumers and this consumption requires labour. During crises of overproduction, employers reduce wages and the number of employees. Goods find fewer buyers. The household reduces expenditures on goods and services and increases labour to compensate for falling incomes. State programs help sustain buying power in the short term but over the longer haul, they do not fill the gap created by lost wages. When the state also cuts back on the proportion of the budget going to social services and limits income support programs, an even heavier burden is placed on the household. Given the sexual division of labour, much of this extra work falls to women.[2]

Thus women are affected not only by their own unemployment or underemployment but also by the unemployment of other family members, which imposes a further burden on women working in the home.

WHO ARE THE UNEMPLOYED?

Nearly 580,000 women were unemployed in 1985, down slightly from the peak of almost 600,000 out of work in 1984. Women accounted for 43% of the unemployed, which was about the same as their representation in the labour force generally. For the decade from 1971 to 1981, the unemployment rate of women was consistently higher than that of men — often by as much as two percentage points — but the reasons for this difference are not clear. Most women are employed in the service sector of the economy, where jobs are more likely to be short-term or temporary, and this may be one possible explanation for women's higher rates of unemployment.

Since 1982, however, the pattern has been reversed, with men's unemployment rates exceeding those of women in 1982 and 1983 (the main recession years) and being slightly lower than women's in 1984 and 1985. Higher unemployment rates for men during the recession undoubtedly reflect the fact that manufacturing and construction industries, where many men are employed, were hit hard by the economic downturn, while service industries fared reasonably well — at least initially.

However, unemployment rates for both women and men are still extremely high by historical standards. Double-digit unemployment rates have prevailed for the past four years, and some forecasts predict rates will exceed 10% through to the end of the decade. In 1985, 10.7% of women workers and 10.3% of men were without work. While this is down from the peak rates of 1983, there were still 578,000 women and 750,000 men out of work in 1985. It is evident that the impact of the recession is still being felt.

The average annual unemployment rates for the provinces differ from the average for Canada as a whole. Residents of the Maritime provinces, Quebec and British Columbia experience more unemployment than the national average, while those in the prairie provinces and Ontario experience less. The rates are shown in Table 3.1.

Unemployment By Age

Jobless rates for young people are very high, with teenagers faring much worse than young adults in the 20- to 24-year age group. In all cases, however, young women seem to be slightly better off than young men are. In 1985, for instance, 16.7% of young women in the 15 to 19 age group were unemployed, compared with 20.6% of young men in the same age group. For 20- to 24-year-olds, the unemployment rate was 13.4% for women and 17.0% for men. Again, the reasons for the difference are not easy to identify. However, one possible explanation is that young women tend to continue longer in education, thereby contributing less to the pool of unskilled workers looking for jobs. Less than 65% of young women in the 15 to 24 age group participated in the work force in 1985, compared with 70% of young men in the same age group.

For older workers, however, the position of women and men is reversed, with 9.4% of women aged 25 and over out of work in 1985, compared with 8.3% of men.

Table 3.1   Unemployment Rates for Canada and the Provinces
Annual Averages, 1985

	Female Rate	Male Rate	Total Rate
	%	%	%
CANADA	10.7	10.3	10.5
Newfoundland	21.1	21.4	21.3
Prince Edward Island	–	12.9	13.2
Nova Scotia	14.2	13.6	13.8
New Brunswick	14.2	16.0	15.2
Quebec	12.1	11.7	11.8
Ontario	8.6	7.6	8.0
Manitoba	8.5	7.9	8.1
Saskatchewan	8.5	7.8	8.1
Alberta	10.1	10.0	10.1
British Columbia	14.1	14.3	14.2

Source: Canada, Statistics Canada, *The Labour Force* (Ottawa: Supply and Services Canada, 1985), table 57, pp. 86-87.

Unemployment By Sector

The occupational segregation of women workers in certain sectors of the economy and in particular occupations is a factor in their unemployment experience. Even in those sectors and occupations thought of as female job ghettos, however, women almost invariably do worse than do men. In the service sector of the economy, where more than 84% of women with paid employment work, the unemployment rate for women in 1985 was 9.1%, compared with 8.4% for men.

Women who worked for various levels of government and for public institutions, such as hospitals and schools, also did poorly in comparison with men. Just over 9% of women working in public administration were unemployed in 1985, compared with 7.7% of men.

In sectors that are non-traditional for women, such as manufacturing, women do much worse than men, with 13.1% of women in manufacturing out of work in 1985, compared with 8.9% of men.

Unemployment By Occupation

In almost every occupational grouping, women's unemployment rates are also higher than men's. In social sciences, 7.6% of women, compared with 5.8% of men, were unemployed in 1985; in teaching, 5.8% of women and 3.0% of men were out of work; in sales occupations, 9.0% of women and 7.3% of men were unemployed; and in clerical jobs, 9.0% of women were out of work, compared to 8.5% of men.

Of even greater concern is evidence that in occupations that might be thought non-traditional for women, and where women compete directly with men, women lose out. In processing, for example, women's unemployment rate was 19.7% in 1985, compared to 10.9% for men; in product fabricating, assembling, and repairing, 14.3% of women and 9% of men were out of work; in materials handling, 18.1% of women and 14.5% of men were unemployed; and in other crafts and equipment operating, 14.4% of women and only 6.6% of men were unemployed in 1985.[3]

The fact that women experience so much higher unemployment rates may be an indication that women's attempts to move into these better-paying, non-traditional jobs have been undermined by the recession and its aftermath. Women may have been the last to be hired and the first to be fired when hard times struck. The data do not present an optimistic picture for women's advancement in the work force.

THE HIDDEN UNEMPLOYED

The official unemployment statistics cited thus far in this chapter underestimate the actual number of unemployed people. Excluded are those who have given up looking for a job, the discouraged workers, as well as part-time workers who would prefer full-time jobs if they could find them.

Discouraged Workers

When jobs are scarce, workers may give up looking because they believe no work is available; these people are not counted as unemployed in the official statistics. At the height of the recession, more than 100,000 workers fell into this category, according to Statistics Canada's measurement. By 1985, there were still 74,000 of these discouraged workers, 49% of them women.

However, the official estimates of the number of discouraged workers leave out another group of women who do not work part-time and are not actively looking for work. These are women with young children who have been unable to find adequate, affordable child care. According to a labour force survey, about 121,000 working mothers had to leave or refuse a job in 1980 because of problems with child care arrangements.[4] Another Canadian study found that many mothers had been forced to quit their jobs because they either could not afford or could not find group care and had found babysitters unreliable.[5] A study from the United States also reported that "lack of child care or inadequate child care keeps women in jobs for which they are overqualified and prevents them from seeking or taking job promotions or the training necessary for advancement."[6]

Maria, a 26-year-old Canadian woman, tells this story: "I've got two kids at home. The day care alone would cost over $800. I'd need to make at least twice that much to make it worth my while to go out and work. Where am I going to find a job that pays over $1,600 a month? You could say I've stopped looking for a job."

Maria has one year of community college training. Before her first child was born in 1978, she worked as a library assistant in the neighbourhood branch of the public library. Now that she is ready to go back to work, the job she used to do is mostly computerized; the women with secure, well-paying jobs at the library branches have Master's degrees in library science. Maria's case is typical of the women who tend to remain the most hidden of the hidden unemployed. For women with small children, the barriers to well-paying employment are multiple. Lack of affordable, quality child care ranks first. Lack of transportation, scarcity of jobs that pay an adequate wage, and employer discrimination against women with small children are also barriers that stand in the way.

Involuntary Part-time Work

"I used to have a full-time job. Now I've been part-time for over two years." Denise is 48: she supports herself and her teenage son, who also works part-time. She is a sales clerk in one of the major department stores. Although she keeps her eye open for full-time work in her local shopping mall, she feels "fairly certain" that, at her age, such jobs will no longer be available to her.

Naomi, aged 31, is a certified teacher of English as a second language. She obtained her certificate in 1978 because she was told it was a "marketable skill". In today's job market, she finds that advice only partially true.

> Teaching in the evenings has become my bread and butter. It's what I know how to do. I'd love to have a full-time job in a community college teaching English as a second language, but I know that's impossible. It's this or more graduate training in a completely different field.

Naomi can work in her chosen field, but only on limited contract terms in the evenings. She does not foresee having a permanent full-time job in the years to come.

Many employers see part-time work as a way of introducing "flexibility" into their work forces. Part-time workers can be called upon to staff businesses during peak hours or times when sales are good. Hourly rates of pay are often less than for those of full-time workers. Part-time workers are usually not eligible for employee benefits such as pension plans and paid sick leave. It is hardly surprising that employers believe part-time workers are a bargain and that they are strongly resisting efforts to give part-time workers a better deal, for example, by including them in employer-sponsored pension plans.

Downsizing and the trend to leaner and meaner management could mean increasing use of part-time workers in the future, instead of the creation of full-time employment, as the economy gradually recovers from recession. Fully 32% of increased employment for women between September 1984 and February 1986, for instance, consisted of part-time work.[7]

The percentage of involuntary part-time workers — those who preferred but could not find full-time work — was up, from 17% in 1980 to 28% in 1985. Thus, 351,000 women who worked part-time in 1985 were part-time workers only because they could not find full-time jobs.[8]

THE DURATION OF UNEMPLOYMENT

The length of time it takes an unemployed worker to find another job rose markedly during the recession. In 1980, for example, unemployment lasted an average of 14.7 weeks (15.0 weeks for men and 14.3 weeks for women). By 1983, the average duration of unemployment had risen to almost 22 weeks.

Even in 1985, however, periods of unemployment lasted much longer than they did five years earlier, indicating that jobs were still very hard to find. The average unemployed worker took 21.6 weeks to find another job. Women experienced shorter unemployment spells than men did, with an average duration of unemployment of 19.7 weeks, compared with 23.1 weeks for men.

As might be expected, women over 45 years of age have much more difficulty finding another job. The average duration of unemployment for women in this age group was 25.7 weeks. However, that still compares favourably with the 32.1 weeks that it took the average unemployed male over the age of 45 to find work.[9]

THE HUMAN CONSEQUENCES OF UNEMPLOYMENT

For anyone who loses a job, some degree of financial hardship may be involved. However, the impact can be devastating for those, including many women, with very low earnings. A single parent, for instance, working at minimum wage and supporting one child on earnings of about $170 a week is already well below the poverty level (estimated at about $260 a week for a family of two living in a large urban area).[10] If she loses her job, she will be entitled to Unemployment Insurance (UI) benefits of 60% of her usual earnings, or $102 a week. However, for the first two weeks in which she is out of work, no benefits are payable. This is the mandatory waiting period provided for under the UI program. If she is out of work for 15 weeks, her UI benefits during that time will average only $88 a week, or about 34% of the poverty level for a family of two.

The maximum UI benefit anyone could receive in 1985, for example, was $276 a week. However, the average benefit being paid to claimants was only $169 a week — a clear indication that many of those without work were at the lower end of the earnings scale.

Apart from the financial hardship of unemployment, and the stress and worry this involves, women are also affected by the unemployment of other family members in ways men often are not. Cathy, a married woman in her thirties, recounts a difficult period in her life:

I was working part-time at the restaurant, and my husband was unemployed for nine months. He was at home all of the time, organizing his calls for jobs, reading the papers, sleeping in every day. I was always trying to help him stay on top of things and keep his spirits up. He wouldn't go out at all to see friends. It was very rough going. The kids would come home and their Dad was very often in a slump or asleep in front of the TV. The strain on me was incredible. I felt like I was keeping the whole show together. I cleaned up after him, made him lunches, cut the grocery bills as much as I could. I was determined to keep our family together. Looking back on it now, I know it took my whole strength to do it.

Making ends meet, both financially and emotionally, is still very much the woman's job in the home. When unemployment for one or both spouses becomes long-term, it is the woman in the household who taps emotional resources to "keep the whole show together". Feelings of guilt, anger and despair, turned inward or outward, are a powerful part of the chronic unemployment picture. The increase in male unemployment has been linked to increased battering of women and children. One Toronto study found that "eighty per cent of wife-beaters reported to Metro Toronto police were unemployed."[11] A study from the United States found that for a 1% increase in the unemployment rate, there was a 2% increase in heart attacks; a 3% to 4% increase in infant mortality; a 4% to 5% increase in suicide and homicide; and a 5% to 6% increase in admission to psychiatric hospitals.[12] According to the Canadian Mental Health Association, unemployment causes an increase in depression, anxiety and mental illness, as well as child abuse, suicide, alcoholism, disease, divorce and crime.[13]

When personal and financial resources are stretched to the breaking point, women as a group are affected particularly severely, as they continue to try to provide mothering, support and household comforts in an atmosphere of tension and strain.

POLICIES TO DEAL WITH UNEMPLOYMENT

Government policies to deal with unemployment have varied with the prevailing conventional wisdom of the economics profession. Until the late 1960s, when the theories of British economist John Maynard Keynes were in vogue, policy focused on stimulating consumer demand through government spending. As consumers, with more money in their pockets to spend, began demanding more goods and services on which to spend it, jobs would be created and unemployment would fall.

By the mid-1970s, however, economic growth dropped sharply, unemployment started to rise, and inflation shot into the double-digit range. Economists, who up to this point had argued that there was a trade-off between unemployment and inflation, were at a loss to explain how the two could exist at the same time. Some pointed to the fact that the composition of the labour force had changed. More women and young people had entered the work force, so more of these workers were now counted among the unemployed. It was argued that since these workers contributed less to total output (because they were assumed to have low skills and therefore low productivity), the economy could not be said to be in trouble until unemployment had reached levels previously considered unacceptable. In other words, these economists argued that women and young people had pushed up the average unemployment rate. They said it was only when the jobless rate of men in their prime earning years (between the ages of 25 and 54) started to rise that policy makers should be concerned.

From the mid-1970s onward, government policy followed the policy prescriptions of the monetarists, led by University of Chicago economist Milton Friedman, who argued that strict control of the money supply is necessary for a healthy economy and that inflation must be wrestled to the ground at any cost. The cost was ever-increasing rates of unemployment. When the recession hit, in the latter half of 1981, unemployment rates began to skyrocket.

By now, economists were putting forward new theories of unemployment, arguing that the problem was not lack of consumer demand leading to lack of jobs but, rather, the characteristics of workers for whom (it was claimed) unemployment is a form of leisure, freely chosen with the assistance of "generous" UI benefits. The implausibility of these theories is striking, yet they form the basis for much of the current criticism of the UI program and for policies being developed to deal with continuing unemployment. Rather than stimulating consumer demand, which would probably have been the policy response in the late 1960s, policies now focus on the supply side. In the belief that the problem is with the supply of workers, measures such as training and retraining programs and incentives encouraging workers to move to other parts of the country where there are greater chances of finding employment are being promoted. Supply-side critics of minimum wages and union pay scales find a willing audience.

The particular and differential impact on women of various policy initiatives has largely been ignored. Many, and perhaps most, economists still base their analyses of the labour market on the behaviour and work patterns of prime-age males, treating all other workers as exceptions to the norm, even though prime-age males accounted for only 38% of all Canadian workers in 1985. Many of the background papers on which the Royal Commission on the Economic Union and Development Prospects for Canada (the Macdonald Commission) based its recommendations dealt with male workers only. It is questionable whether the policy prescriptions of the

Commission, emphasizing adjustment assistance for older workers with long-term attachment to the work force and mobility incentives for unemployed workers, are an appropriate response to women's unemployment.

The systemic bias inherent in economic analysis and economic policy making as it is practised in Canada means that the issue of women's unemployment is not addressed effectively. One brief to the Macdonald Commission, for instance, noted that three of the four largest job creation programs administered by Employment and Immigration Canada in 1983 were directed to increasing employment in sectors dominated by men.[14] For example, the work sharing program under the UI scheme, designed to avoid layoffs, allows employees to work a shorter week while collecting UI benefits. More than three-quarters of the employers involved in the program have been in manufacturing and construction, where male workers predominate. Employment and Immigration Canada reports that 77% of employees taking part in the program in 1982 were men.[15]

The exclusion of women from economic analysis, together with the failure to recognize the unique problems faced by women in the work force, may have serious consequences for women's unemployment in the future. The free trade initiative, for example, now being pursued by negotiators for Canada and the United States, may eventually result in considerable dislocation and loss of jobs. It is generally acknowledged that special assistance will be needed to help the workers most affected by the changes. The Macdonald Commission recognized that many workers would lose their jobs at first. The industries most affected would be textiles, clothing, small electrical products, sporting goods, toys, games, and leather products. About two-thirds of the workers in these six industries are women,[16] many of them immigrants who speak neither of Canada's official languages.

One economist stated recently that most of the workers who would lose their jobs as a result of free trade would be women, but that most of the jobs created would be men's jobs.[17] Rigid occupational segregation of women in the work force may make it particularly difficult for women whose jobs disappear as a result of free trade to be absorbed in newly expanding sectors of the economy, even if the hoped-for increase in employment does eventually materialize.

Policies will need to focus specifically on women's unemployment, but there is little sign yet that this is being contemplated, except in very narrow and traditional ways. Part of the Macdonald Commission's income security proposals, for instance, involve severe cuts in unemployment insurance benefits and their partial replacement with a form of guaranteed annual income. However, the proposal appears to envisage a kind of rationing of jobs, making a distinction between what the Commission calls "employable persons" who would presumably be entitled to benefits and extra assistance to help them adjust to changing labour markets, and what it calls "categories of people whom Canadians do not expect to participate in the labour force", including single parents with young children, who would presumably receive the special guaranteed annual income proposed by the Commission.[18] A background paper prepared for the Commission is much more specific.[19] The author suggests that only those workers certified as employable would be entitled to participate in employment or training programs once their UI benefits (greatly curtailed) had run out. In effect, married women would be denied the right to participate unless their total family income fell below an established level. The author of this paper states that "in the majority of cases, secondary workers in families with another full-time worker would not qualify for special employment."[20]

The possibility of a guaranteed annual income as a replacement for a wide range of social programs is now under discussion by a number of community groups and organizations. As a supplement for the working poor, such a proposal may indeed have merit. There is, however, a very real danger that this initiative may be put forward as an alternative to effective full employment policies and that pressure may be put on women in particular to accept some form of guaranteed income — probably at a very low level — as an alternative to employment. Certainly, this possibility is strongly suggested in some of the work done for the Macdonald Commission. These pressures may be reinforced by the views of those who believe that in times of high unemployment, women should not be "taking jobs away from men". The fact that the jobs women do in the work force — in clerical work, teaching, nursing, and personal service — are not jobs men do anyway seems to have been overlooked by these critics. Pressure on women to return to traditional roles in the home cannot be viewed as the solution to women's unemployment.

ALTERNATIVE OPTIONS

The current policy initiatives of most governments in Canada focus on controlling the money supply, fighting inflation, reducing deficits, and cutting back on government regulation of business. However, alternatives have been proposed that focus directly on unemployment and the need for a full employment policy. The Canadian Labour Congress has adopted a ten-point program for economic recovery, and a book published by the Canadian Centre for Policy Alternatives presents a detailed analysis of an economic strategy for the future.[21]

Contrary to the monetarist approach, these alternatives propose more, rather than less, government involvement in planning the economy for a more secure future. Government spending to stimulate the economy and create jobs is recommended, despite the deficit. From this perspective, unemployment, not the deficit, is public enemy number one, and appropriate government planning and investment based on the country's needs are more likely to produce benefits than is the operation of the marketplace.

48

In this context, there are options to be explored where the likely outcome would be consistent with the full and equal integration of women in the economy. For example, a shorter work week with no loss of pay would be one way to spread the benefits of technology more evenly over the entire population and to share the available paid work. At the same time, it would reduce the double burden of work experienced by many women in the paid labour force and could facilitate the sharing of domestic labour between parents. Expanding, rather than reducing, the public sector and social services would provide more employment for women, since it is in these sectors that many women find work. It would also provide the increased services (such as child care) that support women in participating in the labour force. Special emphasis on training and retraining for women workers would allow a less traumatic transition to automated workplaces. All these options would be strengthened by affirmative action programs, which are necessary to break down the segregation of the labour force and to provide broader employment opportunities for women.

Women's unemployment problems will not be addressed effectively as long as women are excluded from the analysis of economists and policy makers. Many economists still do not acknowledge that women may have a different perception of the economy or may be affected in different ways by economic policies. Also, most do not believe this is an appropriate subject for study. Economists are still prone to dismiss concerns about the economic role of women as "just a social problem". Such biases must be faced and corrected if effective policies are to be developed to deal with the unacceptably high level of unemployment among women.

NOTES

1. There are six Women's Employment Centres in Canada: Vancouver, Calgary, Downsview, Regina, Winnipeg, and Halifax. The centres were established at the beginning of the 1980s.

2. Pat Armstrong, *Labour Pains: Women's Work in Crisis* (Toronto: The Women's Educational Press, 1984), p. 99.

3. Labour force data from Canada, Statistics Canada, *The Labour Force* (Ottawa: Supply and Services Canada, 1985), catalogue no. 71-001.

4. Canada, Statistics Canada, *Labour Force Survey Research Paper No. 31: Initial Results from the 1981 Survey of Child Care Arrangements* (Ottawa: Supply and Services Canada, 1982), table 24, p. 43.

5. Laura C. Johnson and J. Dineen, *The Kin Trade: A Day Care Crisis in Canada* (Toronto: McGraw-Hill Ryerson, 1981).

6. United States, U.S. Commission on Civil Rights, *Child Care and Equal Opportunity for Women*, Clearinghouse Publication No. 67 (Washington, D.C.: 1981), p. 10.

7. Canada, Statistics Canada, *The Labour Force* (Ottawa: Supply and Services Canada, 1984 and 1986). Based on seasonally adjusted data.

8. Canada, Statistics Canada, *Labour Force Annual Averages, 1975-1983* (Ottawa: Supply and Services Canada, 1984), table 32; Canada, Statistics Canada, *The Labour Force* (1985), table 83.

9. Canada, Statistics Canada, *Labour Force Annual Averages, 1975-1983*, table 40; Canada, Statistics Canada, *The Labour Force* (1985), table 91.

10. National Council of Welfare, *1985 Poverty Lines* (Ottawa: Supply and Services Canada, 1985), p. 6. Publication available from National Council of Welfare, Brooke Claxton Building, Ottawa K1A 0K9. (613) 990-8168.

11. Quoted in Pat Armstrong and Hugh Armstrong, "Women and the Economic Crisis", a draft chapter prepared for Meg Luxton and Heather Jon Maroney, ed., *Women's Work, Women's Struggle: Feminism and Political Economy* (Toronto: Methuen, 1987).

12. *Ibid.*

13. Pat Armstrong, *Labour Pains*, p. 106.

14. Pat Armstrong and Hugh Armstrong, "Women and the Economic Crisis", a brief to the Royal Commission on the Economic Union and Development Prospects for Canada (Ottawa: 1983), pp. 23-24.

15. Canada, Employment and Immigration Canada, Program Evaluation Branch, *Evaluation of the Work Sharing Program* (Ottawa: Supply and Services Canada, 1984), table IV, p. 64.

16. Marjorie Cohen, *The Macdonald Report and Its Implications for Women* (Toronto: National Action Committee on the Status of Women, 1985), p. 4.

17. Sunder Magun, "The Effects of Canada-United States Free Trade on the Canadian Labour Market", a conference presented on behalf of the Economic Council of Canada (Winnipeg: Canadian Economic Association Annual Meeting, University of Manitoba, May 29-31, 1986), p. 29.

18. Canada, Royal Commission on the Economic Union and Development Prospects for Canada, *Report*, vol. 2 (Ottawa: Supply and Services Canada, 1985), p. 779.

19. Jonathan R. Kesselman, "Comprehensive Income Security for Canadian Workers", in *Income Distribution and Economic Security in Canada*, François Vaillancourt, research co-ordinator (Toronto: University of Toronto Press for the Royal Commission on the Economic Union and Development Prospects for Canada, 1985).

20. *Ibid.*, p. 295.

21. John Calvert, *Government Limited: The Corporate Takeover of the Public Sector in Canada* (Ottawa: Canadian Centre for Policy Alternatives, 1984).

CHAPTER FOUR

THE UNEMPLOYMENT INSURANCE PROGRAM

In late 1986 and early 1987, two major government-sponsored reports on the Unemployment Insurance (UI) program were issued. They contained proposals that are almost diametrically opposed.

The Commission of Inquiry on Unemployment Insurance (the Forget Commission), which reported in November 1986, recommended radical changes to the program, including a new way of calculating benefits that would mean major cuts in the amount of benefits being paid, particularly in regions of high unemployment.

The House of Commons Standing Committee on Labour, Employment and Immigration (the Hawkes Committee), which reported to Parliament on March 19, 1987, suggested changes that would effectively result in an enhancement of the program, easing the criteria needed to qualify for benefits and instituting a more sympathetic procedure for dealing with claimants. This committee of 11 members of Parliament (7 Progressive Conservatives, 2 Liberals, and 2 NDP) expressed its strong disagreement with the key recommendation of the Forget Commission.

On May 15, 1987, the government made it clear that it intends to take no action to change the UI program at this time. According to the Minister of Employment and Immigration, the Honourable Benoît Bouchard,

> The Government acknowledges Unemployment Insurance is not a perfect program, but the current system is helping millions of Canadians and we will not induce unnecessary uncertainty by attempting change for the sake of change. Our plan is *not* to reduce unemployment insurance but to reduce the *need* for unemployment insurance.

The Canadian Advisory Council on the Status of Women agrees that the primary objective of government policy should be to address the continuing problem of unemployment. As an organization committed to improving the situation of women, we are concerned that on average during 1986, almost 10% of all women in the work force could not find work and that the unemployment rate of women was higher than that of men. In its brief to the Forget Commission, the Council stated:

It is our firm conviction that the continuing high rates of unemployment in Canada must be addressed, not by cutting back financial support to the unemployed, but by developing effective policies for full employment.

In the meantime, however, women continue to face an unacceptably high level of unemployment and will clearly have to continue to rely on the unemployment insurance program to replace a portion of their earnings when they are out of work.

Although the government has chosen to make no changes in the UI program at present, the program is still the subject of debate. There are also particular aspects of the program that concern women and that need attention. In this chapter we review the major proposals of concern to women made by both the Forget Commission and the Hawkes Committee and indicate what actions must be taken to improve the effectiveness of the UI program in meeting women's needs.

THE FORGET COMMISSION

The Commission of Inquiry on Unemployment Insurance came to the conclusion that

[a] fundamental transformation of the design of the Unemployment Insurance program and of the structure of the organization is essential.

However, this view was not shared by all the commissioners. The two representatives of the labour movement, Frances Soboda and Jack Munro, disagreed so strongly with many of the conclusions of the other commissioners that they issued a separate report.

Annualization

The major feature of the majority Forget Commission report was a proposal to change the way UI benefits are calculated. Under the current program, a worker who qualifies for benefits receives 60% of her/his usual weekly earnings, up to a maximum weekly limit. (For 1987, the maximum weekly insurable earnings are $530, so the maximum weekly benefit is 60% of that, or $318.) The "usual weekly earnings" on which the calculation is based are the earnings of the worker in the last 20 weeks before the claim. (For those with less than 20 weeks of employment, earnings of all weeks worked in the year before the claim would be taken into account.) A claimant who has work for 30 weeks before becoming unemployed, for example, would receive benefits at 60% of the average earned during the last 20 weeks worked.

54

Under the Forget Commission's annualization proposal, benefits would be based on the average earnings of the worker for the entire year before the claim, including periods when the worker was unemployed. The following example illustrates how the proposed system would work:

- A worker earns $275 a week for 20 weeks of work and then loses her job. Under the existing system, she would receive 60% of $275, or $165 a week in UI benefits.

- Prior to her current job, this worker had been outside the labour force but looking for work. In the 52-week period before making this claim for UI benefits, she had been able to find work for only 20 weeks. Under the Forget Commission proposal, the UI benefits would be calculated as follows:

1. Her total earnings in the 52 weeks before the claim were $5,500 (that is, 20 weeks x $275).

2. The average weekly earnings on which the UI benefit would be based would be $5,500 divided by 52, or $105.77.

3. Under the Forget proposal, the worker would be entitled to a weekly benefit of 66 2/3% of that amount, or $70.51. (The Forget Commission also proposed an increase in the benefit level from 60% to 66 2/3% of average weekly earnings.)

The benefit level in this example represents only 26% of the worker's usual earnings of $275 a week. A worker who had fewer weeks of employment would get even less in benefits. Someone who worked for only 12 weeks, for example, earning $400 a week before being laid off, would receive benefits of only $61.54 — that is, about 15% of what she was earning before losing her job.

Clearly, the claimants in these cases would not be able to support themselves on the amount of benefits proposed. The Soboda-Munro report points out that under the annualization proposal, more than 62% of claimants would receive less than the $140 a week that welfare pays to a single parent with a child in most provinces. (Under the existing program, 33% of claimants receive less than this amount.)

If annualization were implemented, many claimants would clearly have to resort to social assistance for support if they lost their jobs. Commissioners Soboda and Munro suggest that

[a]nnualization would, in effect, make unemployment insurance irrelevant for a substantial proportion of the unemployed in Canada.

The impact would be catastrophic for individuals, for families, for industries and for regions.

The annualization proposal penalizes workers who cannot find long-term jobs. In effect, only those who have worked for a full 52 weeks before making a UI claim would receive benefits at 66 2/3% of their usual weekly earnings (up to the maximum insurable earnings limit).

For women, annualization could have devastating consequences. A mother on welfare, for example, who is able to enter the work force but loses her job after only a few months, would undoubtedly be forced back on welfare. Women who earn low wages (as many women do) and work in areas of high unemployment where longer-term jobs may not even exist would face the same situation.

Many women in the work force are employed in jobs where wages are low, employee benefits almost non-existent and job security is poor. As the Council pointed out in its brief to the Forget Commission:

> Women workers often have little or no choice as to the kinds of jobs they have in the work force. Occupation segregation, reinforced by systemic discrimination, outlined so clearly in reports such as that of the Royal Commission on Equality in Employment, may prevent them from moving into more stable, better paying jobs in the primary labour market, even when they have the skills and the training to do so.

It is workers in the unstable and low-paying jobs who would be penalized by annualization, and many of them would be women.

The Forget report also recommended the abolition of provisions in the existing program enabling UI claimants in regions of high unemployment to receive benefits for longer than those in other regions. The abolition of these regionally extended benefits, combined with annualization, would result in a reduction in total benefits paid of as much as 56% in Prince Edward Island and 52% in Newfoundland. Benefits to those living in New Brunswick would be cut by 49%, while benefits paid in Alberta would drop by only 23%.

The Earnings Supplementation Proposal

To compensate for the major cutbacks in benefits it recommends, the Forget Commission suggested a federal earning supplementation program, which, it said, could be boosted by provincial supplements. The whole system would be implemented following federal-provincial discussions, which the Commission said "should probably result in bilateral or multilateral agreements."

The earnings supplementation program would be directed at the working poor. According to the Commission,

> An earnings supplementation plan should improve the options open to a person struggling to establish self-sufficiency through participation in the labour force.

However, the earnings supplement to the working poor would be based on total household income rather than individual income. This would have major implications for women. Although by virtue of their individual earnings, many women can be considered "working poor", a woman's right to an earnings supplement to augment her low wages would depend on the income of other family members.

The consequences would be twofold:

1. Women would be forced back into a situation of dependency within the family unit. Women who now receive UI benefits as a matter of right, based on their own earnings and contributions as individual workers in the paid labour force, would find these benefits cut off and replaced with an income- or means-tested benefit (the earnings supplementation program) where their right to benefits would be determined not by their own financial situation, but by that of someone else. We can safely assume that in most cases, it would be that of their husbands.

2. The second consequence relates to the nature of women's participation in the work force. As we have noted, many women in the paid labour force are confined to low-wage job ghettoes. In addition, 62% of all the women in the Canadian work force in 1986 were married women. Because most married women earn very much less than their husbands, most would probably not qualify for the earnings supplement. It seems evident that the "person struggling to establish self-sufficiency through participation in the labour force" whom the Forget Commission had in mind for earnings supplementation would, in most cases, be male.

The Entrance Requirement

Under the existing program, those who claim regular UI benefits must have 10 to 14 weeks of employment (known as the entrance requirement) in the 52 weeks before their claim, depending on the unemployment rate in the region where they live. But new entrants or re-entrants to the work force and claimants for maternity or adoption benefits must have worked for 20 weeks in the 52-week period before their claim to qualify for benefits. Because women's work patterns may be different from those of men, and because it is only women who can claim maternity benefits, the longer qualifying periods are more likely to affect women than men. The Council objected when the longer entrance requirement for new entrants, re-entrants, repeaters and part-time workers was introduced in 1979, on the grounds that these provisions discriminated against women.

The rationale advanced by policy makers for the longer entrance requirements has always been that people just entering the work force, or re-entering after a period away from paid employment, as well as those who claim maternity benefits, must demonstrate that they are truly attached to the work force before they can be allowed UI coverage. (The systemic bias is obvious here, of course, since the implication is that women are not really serious about working for pay and many enter the work force simply to get UI benefits.)

The Forget Commission said that since annualization would be based on a claimant's earnings during the entire 52 weeks before a claim, there would be no need to require certain claimants to have worked longer than others to establish their eligibility for benefits. In other words, annualization would penalize those with less attachment to the work force by giving them lower benefits. Accordingly, the Forget report proposed that the entrance requirement for eligibility would be 350 hours of work for everyone in all regions. To be eligible for benefits, all claimants, whether for regular or special benefits (such as maternity and adoption) would have to have accumulated at least 350 hours of employment, equivalent to about 10 weeks of work, during the 52 weeks before a claim.

While we support a uniform entrance requirement for all claimants, we cannot support the linking of this to annualization, for the reasons already outlined.

The Cumulative Employment Account

In making this proposal, the Forget Commission also fails to recognize that there would be a differential effect on women. In fact, the cumulative employment account proposal is a perfect example of systemic discrimination. The objective of the account would be to increase benefits for long-service workers by allowing them to build up credits for past service; they could draw on this additional UI entitlement if they later became unemployed. But the proposed design of the program is such that it would almost certainly exclude many women workers.

A worker would be given a credit of two weeks of UI benefits for each full year worked, but the account could not be drawn on until the worker had completed 30 years of employment. The maximum that could be accrued in the account would provide for one additional year of UI benefits. The Forget report suggests that workers might draw on their cumulative employment accounts to top up benefits if they were laid off after many years of service, or to support themselves while they undertook training or upgrading or moved to another part of the country to look for work.

The Commission rejected the idea of making this benefit available to all workers over a certain age. Apart from the fact that this might have contravened the Charter of Rights and Freedoms, age "is not necessarily a good indicator of long-term attachment to the labour force," the Commission said. Unless the benefit is tied to long-term labour force attachment, workers might "enter the labour force simply to collect benefits." At least ten years' attachment to the work force would have to be required, said the report.

While the language is carefully neutral, the bias is clear. The implications of this kind of proposal for women are obvious. It takes no account of the possibility that women's work patterns may differ from men's. Because of their childbearing and family responsibilities, many women may not have the requisite long-term, uninterrupted attachment to the work force, even though they may be long-term labour force participants.

Many women, too, may have had to re-enter the work force at a later stage in their lives as the result of divorce or the death of a spouse. Yet older women workers who lose their jobs may find it just as difficult as older men to get the retraining they need or to find other employment if they lose their jobs. (Some may even find it more difficult.) Many of these women may be the sole support of themselves or their families and could face serious hardship if unemployed. The design of the cumulative employment account seems tailor-made for the long-term male worker and almost intentionally excludes women workers. It fails to acknowledge that most women now participate in the work force for most of their lives, but that most still also have to shoulder the major responsibility for care of children and other family members.

Maternity, Parental, and Adoption Benefits

In the area of maternity, parental and adoption benefits, the Forget Commission appeared to be much more sensitive to the needs of women. The UI program should continue to provide coverage for these eventualities, the Commission said.

> This is in keeping with the definition of unemployment as resulting from either job loss or a temporary interruption of earnings. It is just as reasonable to cover temporary sickness and maternity periods as it is to cover temporary lay-offs with recall notices.

The Commission recommended a two-tier system of maternity and parental benefits made up of

- maternity benefits available during the period surrounding childbirth; and

- parental benefits available during the period following maternity leave or placement of an adopted child.

Parental benefits should be available to either or both parents (but not concurrently), such that the total amount of benefits does not exceed the maximum available to one parent; this should be made available only to those who are active labour force participants.

The Commission also proposed the removal of the current 15-week limit on the combined total of sickness and maternity/adoption benefits so that the availability of sickness benefits would be separate and distinct from any maternity or parental benefits to which a person is entitled. The Council recommended this change in its brief to the Commission.

The Council was disappointed to note that the Commission recommended the retention of the two-week waiting period before maternity or parental benefits become payable. Since a mother (or father) who claims these benefits cannot be expected to be available or looking for work, we see no justification for requiring her to forgo benefits for the first two weeks of her leave period.

We also find it difficult to understand why the Forget Commission recommended that the total benefit period of 15 weeks be maintained. Its proposals for allowing the father to share in this benefit immediately following the birth are inconsistent with the changes to the Canada Labour Code introduced in 1984. The Code now provides a statutory right for women to take 17 weeks of maternity leave, followed by a further

24 weeks of unpaid leave, which may be taken by either parent, to care for a newborn or newly adopted child.

The Council has taken the position that some portion of the leave following the birth of a child should be reserved for the mother to allow for her physical recuperation from childbirth. Although the Forget Commission does not specify how long the maternity leave proposed as part of its first tier of maternity and parental benefits should be, it seems reasonable that UI maternity and parental benefits should follow the pattern already established by the Canada Labour Code, that is, the first 17 weeks of leave (assuming the abolition of the two-week waiting period) to be available to the mother and a further period of 24 weeks to be available to either parent. This implies that parental benefits under the UI program would eventually be extended from the current 17 weeks. We see no reason why a gradual lengthening of the benefit period could not be phased in over time.

Inclusion of Part-time Workers

In our brief to the Forget Commission, we referred to the finding of the federal Commission of Inquiry Into Part-time Work that 40% of part-time workers work less than 15 hours a week and so are not covered by UI. (The existing program requires that an employee work a minimum of 15 hours a week or earn at least 20% of the maximum weekly insurable earnings — equivalent to about $106 in 1987 — to be eligible for coverage.) Since more than 71% of all part-time workers are women, this is an issue of particular concern.

The Forget report recommends extending UI coverage to all part-time workers, but first of all to those who work a minimum of eight hours a week. It said that workers should be allowed to accumulate hours of work in order to become eligible for coverage; it also suggested that the Canada Employment and Immigration Commission look further into the feasibility of covering all hours of work, including work for different employers.

Although these recommendations appear progressive, it must be emphasized that under the Commission's annualization proposal, eligibility for UI benefits would be based on a minimum entrance requirement of 350 hours of work in the previous 52 weeks. A part-time worker who regularly worked only eight hours a week would thus have to be employed at that rate for 44 weeks before being covered by the program.

Under the existing program, part-time workers (that is, those working more than 15 hours a week) need work for only 10 to 14 weeks to qualify for regular benefits (15 to 20 weeks if they are new entrants or re-entrants to the work force). Under the Forget proposal, a part-time worker who worked 15 hours a week would have to be employed for about 23 weeks (equivalent to 350 hours) before being covered by the program.

THE STANDING COMMITTEE ON LABOUR, EMPLOYMENT AND IMMIGRATION

This standing committee of the House of Commons, chaired by Jim Hawkes, MP, examined the UI program and heard testimony from a number of witnesses. It reported to Parliament on March 19, 1987. The Committee disagreed totally with the concept of annualization, which, it said,

> would create undue hardship and increase the costs of other social programs; would adversely affect both the long-term and short-term labour market objectives of Unemployment Insurance; and would be totally at variance with the concept of pooling risks within a social insurance program.

It also disagreed with the Forget Commission's proposal to drop regionally extended benefits and to tighten up entrance requirements. In contrast, the Committee recommended that regardless of where they live, claimants should have to work only 10 weeks (instead of the current 10 to 14 weeks) to qualify for full benefits. The benefit level should remain at 60% of insured earnings, said the Committee, but the possibility of increasing it to 66 2/3% should be explored by a new autonomous Unemployment Insurance Commission, which it recommended be established to deliver the UI program.

The Committee made several recommendations of significance to women. Many of them reflect recommendations already adopted by the Council.

- That the two-week waiting period for maternity/adoption benefits be eliminated. (The Council recommended the abolition of the waiting period as long ago as 1976.)

- On entrance requirements, the Committee recommended that new entrants and re-entrants to the work force, and those who claim special benefits such as for maternity or adoption, not have to work longer than other workers to qualify for benefits. (This is in line with the Council's recommendations, described earlier.)

- That a minimum of six hours work in a week (not necessarily in a single job) entitle a worker to one week of benefits; that the minimum insurable earnings requirement be eliminated; and that people who hold more than one job be able to count all their earnings from all jobs as insured earnings entitling them to benefits.

62

These proposals would address the needs of part-time workers and are in line with the Council's recommendations, first made in 1983 and 1984, that eligibility requirements for part-time workers be amended to ensure that a much higher proportion of part-time workers have access to UI.

■   That credit banking be extended to people who leave the labour force temporarily for reasons such as schooling, child rearing, or serving Canada abroad as workers or spouses of workers. Credit banking is a provision in the current program that allows workers who find a full-time job to suspend their claim and take it up again later if they lose the job, rather than terminate the claim and have to qualify for a new claim later if the job does not work out.

This proposal would clearly be advantageous to women workers and is one we support.

■   On maternity/adoption benefits, the Hawkes Committee believed that sickness, maternity and adoption benefits are legitimate and distinctly separate insurable contingencies; it was also conscious of a possible need for separate parental benefits. However, it said it had reservations about the appropriate method of delivery and financing.

On this point, we believe it would be feasible to deliver and expanded program of parental benefits through the UI program. Apart from the fact that administrative structures are already in place that could easily be adapted to an expanded program, there are constitutional reasons for leaving such benefits under the aegis of the UI program. These were outlined in our brief to the Forget Commission.

        We would like to see policy development move in this direction, and we were disappointed at the apparent reluctance of the Hawkes Committee to recommend an expansion of the current maternity benefits program, beyond advocating the elimination of the initial two-week waiting period. In line with this proposal, the Committee recommended that maternity and adoption benefits be paid for a maximum of 17 weeks, instead of the current 15. It proposed, as did the Forget Commission, that sickness and maternity benefits could be taken consecutively, instead of limiting claimants to a total of 15 weeks of special benefits (sickness and maternity together) as the current program does. As well, the Committee said that eligible claimants should not be disentitled from receiving sickness, maternity or adoption benefits during an industrial dispute, as they are now. This is also a recommendation we support.

        The Committee recommended that the new Unemployment Insurance Commission be asked to study the possibility of providing parental benefits in addition to the maternity/adoption benefits now available under the program. One other proposal in this area that the Council also favours was that if a child is hospitalized while the parent is receiving maternity or adoption benefits, the balance of the special benefits claim could be banked and reactivated when the child is released from hospital.

The Committee also emphasized that sickness, maternity and adoption benefits are legitimate insurable risks within the concept of social insurance and should therefore continue to be funded by the premiums paid by employers and employees, not from the general revenues of the government — a view with which we concur.

■ That under all circumstances, clients be treated with dignity and respect. Several changes in the way the program is administered were proposed to meet this objective. In particular, the Committee said, when it comes to job search requirements,

> there should be an initial presumption that, without objective evidence to the contrary, claimants will generally seek and accept employment based on reasonable expectations as to what is or will become available...

> That there be an initial presumption of trust regarding the claimant's availability for work... The officer's primary responsibility should be to advise and assist claimants.

We welcome these recommendations and would like to see them implemented to benefit all claimants, women and men.

■ On the question of workers who voluntarily quit their jobs without just cause, the Committee said that objective criteria as to what constitutes just cause should be spelled out in the UI regulations and should include, among others, sexual harassment, discrimination, occupational health and safety reasons, and accompanying a spouse who is moving to a new job. All claimants should be made fully aware of these criteria, said the Committee, and great care should be taken to ensure that the wording is accurate and free from the possibility of subjective interpretation.

These recommendations are clearly of great importance for women. Indeed, the Council adopted similar recommendations in December 1985. However, we suggest that problems with child care arrangements should also be included in the list of just causes for which a worker may have to quit a job.

■ The Committee also recommended that employed spouses be eligible for UI coverage, provided they are not treated as a partner in the business, but as an employee. This proposal goes some way to meeting our concerns about coverage for women who work in family businesses with their spouses. The Committee said that in the coming months, it intends to examine the issue of including all self-employed people in the UI program.

THE GOVERNMENT'S RESPONSE

The federal government's response to these two widely differing views of the Unemployment Insurance program has been to choose the path of least resistance and to do nothing. We believe that decision is a mistake.

We do not believe, however, that radical reform of the UI program is needed at this time. The scope of the sweeping changes envisioned by the Forget Commission is reflected in the fact that if its recommendations were implemented, benefits would be cut by about $3 billion. Such a massive restructuring of the program would have devastating consequences for the unemployed and, in our view, would be totally unacceptable. With unemployment rates still well above 9% we urge the federal government to make stronger efforts to deal with the problem of unemployment and not to contemplate any reduction of benefits to those without work.

The more modest proposals of the Hawkes Committee represent a housecleaning of the UI program, which we feel is long overdue and could easily be implemented at this time. The cost of these proposals has been estimated at $180 million, which we do not see as unreasonable.

We believe it is significant that the report of the House of Commons Standing Committee on Labour, Employment and Immigration represents the unanimous view of 11 members of Parliament from all three political parties. Subject to the reservations outlined earlier in this chapter, we concur with their view of the kinds of changes to the Unemployment Insurance program that are needed at this time.

As far as women are concerned, there are changes that would be relatively simple to implement and that we believe should be put in place without delay. Those changes are outlined below:

■ **Part-time workers.** Many of the jobs created over the past few years have been part-time jobs. (Between 1984 and 1986, 26% of new jobs for women were part-time jobs.) The vast majority of part-time workers are women, but an increasing percentage of those who work part-time do so because they have been unable to find the full-time employment they would prefer. Wages of part-time workers make a vital contribution to the income of their families. We believe these workers should have the same protection against interruptions in earnings through unemployment as other workers in the labour force. We urge the government to change the minimum hours criteria for UI coverage so that more part-time workers are covered by the program.

■ **Maternity and parental benefits.** A number of changes should be made to the program now. Other reforms could be phased in gradually. As immediate changes we would like to see:

1. dropping of the two-week waiting period for maternity and adoption benefits, so that eligible claimants would receive benefits for 17 weeks instead of the current 15;

2. elimination of the provision that maternity and adoption benefits will not be paid to claimants during an industrial dispute;

3. elimination of the provision that a claimant may receive a total of only 15 weeks sickness and maternity/adoption benefits combined. These types of benefits should be treated separately, so that a claimant who receives sickness benefits before making a maternity or adoption benefit claim should not be deprived of a full 17 weeks of maternity or adoption benefits when she becomes eligible for them; and

4. reduction of the entrance requirement for maternity, adoption and sickness benefits so that claimants for these benefits do not have to work longer than other UI claimants who qualify.

In the longer term, we would like to see an increase in the level of benefits provided for maternity and adoption so that those who take this leave do not suffer such a severe financial penalty as a result of their childbearing and child rearing responsibilities; an extension of the benefit period from the current 17 weeks to bring benefits into line with the statutory leave provisions of the Canada Labour Code; and a provision that parents (fathers as well as mothers) may share the benefits at their discretion, with the proviso that a period of benefits immediately following the birth of a child should be reserved for the mother only.

■ **New entrants and re-entrants.** Reduction of the entrance requirements for these workers so that they do not have to work longer than other workers to qualify for benefits.

■ **Voluntary quits.** Clear criteria, embodied in the UI regulations, defining what constitutes just cause for voluntarily quitting a job. The criteria should include sexual harassment, discrimination, occupational health and safety reasons, accompanying a spouse moving to a new job, and breakdown of child care arrangements.

The proposals are not new. Most have long been advocated by the Canadian Advisory Council on the Status of Women. Some were recommended at least six years ago by a Task Force that looked a the UI program then. We believe there would be wide public support for these changes and we are encourage that Members of Parliament from all three political parties have recommended them. It is now time for the government to act.

CHAPTER FIVE

ARE WE PROTECTED? EMPLOYMENT STANDARDS LEGISLATION

The large majority — 68% — of women in paid employment are not unionized. For these women, basic standards for hours of work, wages, vacation, holidays, and notice of dismissal are defined by employment standards legislation. Given the low rate of unionization among women and the low-paid, unskilled jobs in which many women are employed, the minimal provisions of employment standards legislation often reflect the actual conditions of work for many women.

Moreover, unionization is no guarantee that benefits will exceed the legislated minimum. While most unions negotiate pay rates above the minimum wage, many unionized workers have negotiated provisions for other benefits that do not exceed those provided under employment standards legislation. For example, in Quebec, collective agreements covering establishments employing 500 or more workers include a total of 555,000 workers. Sixteen per cent of these unionized workers have no provision for statutory holidays, 28% have the same vacation allowance as provided in the legislation (two weeks after one year of employment), and 49% have no provision for notice of individual layoff.[1] The fact that unionized workers are unable to obtain benefits that exceed the legislated minimum indicates the importance legislation has in setting basic standards for all workers, unionized and non-unionized.

This chapter outlines the major provisions of the legislation in the 13 jurisdictions, that is, the 10 provinces, the Northwest Territories, the Yukon, and the federal jurisdiction. Maternity leave and equal pay are excluded, since they are dealt with elsewhere in this book. Certain specific groups of women workers are considered, because they have less protection under the law than other workers do.

HOURS OF WORK, VACATIONS AND HOLIDAYS

In the context of the recent economic climate, high unemployment and technological change, legislated provisions concerning daily, weekly and yearly work hours take on a new significance. One method of providing paid work for more people is to reduce the standard number of hours of work so that more jobs are created. Employment standards legislation establishes weekly hours of work, regulates overtime, and sets the length of paid vacations and the number of statutory holidays.

All jurisdictions set the number of hours to be worked in a standard or normal work week (except for New Brunswick, which at present has no provisions limiting hours of work). If more hours are worked, overtime must be paid at the rate of one-and-a-half times the regular wage. The standard work week is the shortest, at 40 hours, in British Columbia, Manitoba, Saskatchewan, the Yukon and the federal jurisdiction. In six jurisdictions (Alberta, Newfoundland, Northwest Territories, Ontario and Quebec) the standard work week is 44 hours, and in Nova Scotia and Prince Edward Island it is 48 hours.

Thus, while 40 hours per week is often considered the norm for full-time employment, in most jurisdictions the legislated maximum is above 40 hours per week. On the other hand, the average hours worked by women in 1985 in their main full-time job was 38.8 hours;[2] this indicates that much of the legislation is out of touch with the reality of women's hours of paid work.

The amount of overtime worked becomes a concern in times of high unemployment. It can be argued that overtime should be limited or entirely prohibited in circumstances where job creation is a priority.[3] Seven of the 13 jurisdictions establish maximum hours beyond which workers must not be required to work, even on overtime. The strongest restrictions on overtime are in Manitoba, where the standard and the maximum work week are both set at 40 hours per week. Workers may be required to work overtime only "where work is urgently required to maintain or repair equipment or plant, in the event of an occurrence beyond human control which affects the life, health or safety of individuals or which interrupts the provision of an essential service."[4]

Saskatchewan sets the maximum hours of work at 44. In Ontario and the federal jurisdiction, it is 48 hours, in the Northwest Territories, 54 hours and in the Yukon, 60 hours per week. The longest maximum hours of work are in Newfoundland, at 16 hours per day. In the remaining six provinces (British Columbia, Alberta, New Brunswick, Quebec, Nova Scotia and Prince Edward Island), no maximum hours are established, so that overtime is unlimited under the employment standards provisions of these provinces.

However, even where there is a maximum, the practical application of the law does not mean that those hours are absolute. Where a maximum is set, employers can still request, though not require, that a worker put in longer hours. A worker who wants to refuse the excess hours may have to lay a complaint with an employment standards officer to have those rights respected. Moreover, most jurisdictions have permit systems to allow employers to exceed the maximums. These permits are usually awarded to employers routinely and without question.

All jurisdictions have legislation that deals with the length of vacations, vacation pay, and entitlement periods. The most generous provisions are in Saskatchewan, where workers are entitled to three weeks of paid vacation after a year of employment, rising to four weeks after ten years. In every other jurisdiction, only two weeks of vacation are provided after the first year of work. The vacation period rises to three weeks after four years in Manitoba; after five years in British Columbia and the Northwest Territories; and after six years in the federal jurisdiction. In Quebec a worker must wait ten years in order to qualify for three weeks' vacation.

The greater the wait for a longer vacation, the fewer the number of workers who qualify, particularly among women who take breaks from employment for family responsibilities. In 1985, 40% of employed women had held their present jobs for more than five years, compared with 52% of men.[5] However, in six jurisdictions, the legislated vacation period never increases beyond two weeks. Legislated vacation provision in Canada is low compared to many European countries. Three weeks are provided in Hungary; 18 days in West Germany; four weeks in Austria, Belgium, and France; five weeks in Sweden; and six weeks in Denmark.[6]

With the sole exception of Prince Edward Island, all jurisdictions have provisions for time off, or overtime pay in lieu of time off, for a number of statutory holidays. Newfoundland has five statutory holidays; Nova Scotia and New Brunswick have six; Ontario and Quebec have seven; Alberta and Manitoba have eight, and the other five jurisdictions have nine. Where a worker is required to work on a holiday, most jurisdictions require that the pay for that day be one-and-a-half times the regular pay; in Quebec, a worker must receive double-time pay or another day off within three weeks of the holiday.

Provision for sick leave is legislated only in the federal jurisdiction and the Yukon. Since January 1985, a worker in the Yukon may not be dismissed or laid off for an unpaid absence resulting from illness or injury of up to one day per month, with a maximum of six days per year. However, legislated minimums for sick leave with pay do not exist in Canada; nor do provisions for educational leave or leave to care for sick relatives. These and other provisions are legislated in other countries. In Germany, 6 weeks' paid sick leave are provided; in Belgium workers have a right to 240 hours per year of paid educational leave for vocational training; in Austria one week per year is provided for the care of sick relatives; in Hungary additional vacation leave is provided to parents, varying according to the number and ages of their children.[7]

NOTICE OF TERMINATION AND UNJUST DISMISSAL

Losing one's job is usually a traumatic experience, involving financial uncertainty, searching for other work, and real hardship if income drops substantially, especially if there is a dependent family. In most jurisdictions, the only requirement placed upon employers when they dismiss workers is to provide some advance notice of termination, although in the Northwest Territories, employers are not yet obligated even to this extent, and in New Brunswick only workers not covered by a collective agreement receive notice of termination under the statute law. Under common (or unwritten) law, anyone can sue an employer for lack of reasonable notice, but workers not covered by statute law in the Northwest Territories and New Brunswick do not have access to the statutory enforcement provisions, as described later in this chapter. All the other jurisdictions do require the employer to give advance notice of termination where an individual worker is involved.

A worker has to be employed for a certain period before notice of termination is required. This period varies from two weeks in Manitoba to six months in British Columbia and New Brunswick, but is most commonly three months. Until this period of employment is completed, a worker has no right to any notice and may legally be dismissed on the spot. Where notice must be given, the most common requirement is for just one week of advance notice. British Columbia, New Brunswick, and the federal jurisdiction are somewhat more generous, providing two weeks.

In British Columbia, Ontario, New Brunswick, Nova Scotia, Quebec and Saskatchewan, the required notice increases with length of employment, up to a maximum of eight weeks after eight to ten years of employment, depending on the province. However, in Prince Edward Island, no more than one week of notice is ever required; Alberta, Newfoundland, and the federal jurisdiction provide no more than two weeks; and in Manitoba the normal pay period is the period of required notice. Thus, the amount of notice can be very limited.

When a group of workers is dismissed at the same time, alternative work may be harder to find; in addition, the community at large may be affected, particularly in smaller towns and single-industry towns. In this situation, the required periods of notice are longer, but legislation governing group terminations exists in only 8 of the 13 jurisdictions. Under the federal jurisdiction, an employer is required to provide 16 weeks' notice where 50 or more workers' jobs are terminated. In Manitoba, Newfoundland, Nova Scotia, Ontario, Quebec and the Yukon, the period of notice varies from 8 to 16 weeks, depending on the number of jobs to be terminated. New Brunswick provides for only 4 weeks of notice where 25 or more jobs are terminated, and this applies only to workers covered by a collective agreement.

Severance pay — a lump-sum payment to a worker who loses a job — provides some temporary financial security in a situation where regular earnings cease. Only two jurisdictions provide any such security. Under federal legislation, a worker employed for at least 12 continuous months must receive two days' wages for every year of work completed and

72

a minimum of five days' wages. In Ontario, severance pay is required when the employer terminates the employment of at least 50 workers within a period of six months. The payment is then one week of regular pay for every year of employment. These are the only arrangements for severance pay under employment standards legislation.

Finally, protection against unjust dismissal is provided under employment standards legislation in only three jurisdictions and applies only to certain workers. Under the federal act, a worker must have been employed for 12 months, in Quebec for 5 years, and in Nova Scotia for 10 years before being eligible to make an appeal under the legislation. A worker anywhere in Canada can launch a civil case on the grounds of wrongful dismissal and obtain financial compensation, but only in the three jurisdictions with statutory provisions may the worker be reinstated if the complaint is upheld. Without such provisions in law, the courts have always refused to consider reinstatement as a remedy. Moreover, the existence of the legislation may in itself act as a deterrent to unjust dismissal.

MINIMUM WAGES

Minimum wage legislation is in force in all jurisdictions, the objective being to set a floor below which wages cannot fall. As of March 1986, the wage set for adult workers varied from a low of $3.50 an hour, under the federal jurisdiction, to $4.50 an hour in Saskatchewan.

Statistics Canada establishes low-income lines, and it is generally agreed that people with incomes below these lines are living in poverty. The lines vary according to family size and place of residence (rural or urban). In 1985, the lines for a single person varied from $7,571 in a rural area to $10,238 in a city of half a million people or more. For a two-person family, the line varied from $9,895 to $13,508. It is not necessary to quote the lines for three- or four-person families, because not one of the minimum wage rates comes close to meeting them.

Even the highest minimum wage rate — $4.50 in Saskatchewan — would generate an income of only $9,360 for a year of full-time employment. This is insufficient for one person to live above the poverty line in an urban area, and a family of two people or more would fall below the poverty line no matter where they lived. In other words, most single people and all families dependent on a minimum wage income in any jurisdiction are living in poverty. Although employment standards legislation establishes a minimum rate, it clearly makes no attempt to set an adequate one.

Minimum wage rates are not indexed to inflation but are raised on an ad hoc basis. At the time of writing, the minimum wage had not been raised for three years in New Brunswick and the Northwest Territories; for four years in Alberta, Quebec, and the federal jurisdiction; and for five years in British Columbia. Inflation eats away at the value of the minimum wage, putting minimum wage workers further and further below the poverty line.

How many workers are paid at minimum wage rates? The most recent information is for December 1984, from a special survey by Statistics Canada. At that time, three provinces had an adult minimum wage rate of $4: Manitoba, Ontario, and Quebec. The proportion of workers earning at or below $4 an hour was 9% in Manitoba, 10% in Quebec, and 12% in Ontario. (Each of these provinces has lower minimum wage rates for young workers and students, set at that time at below $4 an hour.) The figures show that the proportion of women working at or below the adult minimum wage rate is significantly higher than the proportion of men. Thus, in Manitoba, 11% of employed women worked at or below $4 an hour, compared to 7% of men; in Quebec, the figures are 14% of women, compared to 7% of men; and in Ontario, 16% of women, compared to 9% of men.[8]

ENFORCEMENT

Under common law, any person may take a civil case through regular court procedures to recover unpaid wages. Whether it concerns regular pay, holiday or vacation pay, overtime, pay in lieu of notice, or severance pay, such amounts may be claimed before the courts as unpaid debts previously contracted by the employer. However, taking a case to court may be an expensive and lengthy procedure, and all jurisdictions provide an alternative course of action under the legislation.

In offices across the country that administer employment standards legislation, trained officials are available to receive complaints. In general, these officials are empowered to investigate situations and to attempt to reach an amicable settlement between the workers and the employer. If this proves impossible, the official in most cases may order the employer to pay compensation and may file the order in a court, making it enforceable as a judgement of that court.

In most jurisdictions, taking a civil action or using the statutory recourse are mutually exclusive methods of recovering payment obligations from the employer. However, there are some important exceptions and limitations. In Nova Scotia and Prince Edward Island, the statutory recourse must be used to enforce the statutory obligations of an employer, but these include all wages and commissions, not just the minimum wage. In these two provinces, civil action may be used only to recover amounts that are not required by law but are due under the employment contract, such as severance pay. In four provinces, limits are set on the amount that may be claimed through the statutory recourse: one year's wages in Manitoba, $4,000 in Ontario, $2,000 in Prince Edward Island, and twice the minimum

74

wage in Quebec. In these cases, if the worker's claim to unpaid wages exceeds these limits, civil action is necessary to obtain any amount above the established limit.

Often, the intervention of an employment standards official is sufficient to produce a settlement, and in such situations the statutory recourse is faster and cheaper than any civil action could be. However, where amicable agreement cannot be reached and a more formal procedure must be instituted, delays and costs may increase accordingly. For example, in a case in Quebec, a worker fired after 22 years on the job complained to the Commission. After mediation failed, an arbitration hearing was held, for which the worker had to hire a lawyer and share the cost of the arbitrator. The worker finally won her case, but it was 18 months after she had been fired, during which time she had incurred $7,000 in expenses and undergone a great deal of stress. She was awarded $10,000 in compensation.[9]

In all jurisdictions, workers filing a complaint against an employer are protected under the legislation. It is illegal to dismiss a worker for instituting procedures under employment standards legislation, and employers may be subject to criminal sanctions, fines, and imprisonment for violating the law. However, despite these protections, workers may still be fearful of initiating complaints against their employers, especially in periods of high unemployment when other jobs may be scarce.

WOMEN NOT PROTECTED BY THE LAWS

Although the employment standards described above are limited in the protection they provide, there are nonetheless groups of workers that are excluded from even these minimums, or that receive only reduced coverage. Women make up a large proportion of these groups.

Part-time and Temporary Workers

Women account for 72% of all part-time workers, and 26% of women employed in 1985 held part-time positions.[10] Many women work part-time in order to balance child care responsibilities with paid work. However, the number of part-time workers who are thus employed because they cannot find full-time jobs has been increasing; 28% of women in part-time work would prefer full-time jobs.[11] With the exception of some professional and highly unionized occupations, most part-time jobs are low-paying, offer little opportunity for advancement, and rarely provide benefits equal to those of full-time workers.

Part-time workers are sometimes excluded from the protection employment standards laws can offer, either directly through legislation or indirectly because they have insufficient hours of work to meet the requirements necessary to obtain benefits or protections. In British Columbia, part-time instructors are excluded from any coverage under employment standards legislation, as are domestics in Manitoba and Ontario who work less than 24 hours per week.

In New Brunswick and Prince Edward Island, workers employed for less than 24 hours per week are excluded from vacation rights and are entitled to neither time off nor vacation pay. Moreover, a worker must work 19 days in each calendar month in New Brunswick and 90% of the working time of the establishment in Prince Edward Island to obtain vacation time, clearly excluding the vast majority of part-time workers (though they would still receive 4% additional pay in lieu of vacation time). Nova Scotia also has a minimum working time provision based on the prevalent working hours in the establishment, thereby excluding many part-time workers from access to vacation time.

In most jurisdictions, it is common to require employees to work a certain number of days prior to a statutory holiday in order to be eligible to receive the holiday off with pay. In four jurisdictions, a worker must have earned wages for 15 of the 30 calendar days prior to the holiday. Consequently, part-time workers employed for three days per week or less would not qualify for paid holidays.

In 1983, a federal government task force suggested the specific inclusion of part-time workers in the legislation. It was recommended that, over a four-year period, the federal government introduce "a new labour standard which would ensure that part-time workers are included in all fringe benefit and pension plans (on a pro-rated basis) where an employer provides these benefits for full-time workers doing similar work."[12] In 1984, the federal government changed its provisions; workers who work less than 15 days in the 30 days preceding the holiday receive holiday pay pro-rated at one-twentieth of the wages earned in the previous 30 days.

On January 1, 1987, federal legislation came into effect allowing part-time workers under federal jurisdiction who earn more than 35% of the average industrial wage for two consecutive years to join private pension plans. One of the problems with this legislation, however, is that it tends to favour men who work part-time because men's wages generally exceed women's wages, while the calculation of the average industrial wage includes both men's and women's wages.

Many part-time workers are also temporary workers; in 1985, 28% of all employed women had held their jobs for less than a year, while 12% had been in their current positions for three months or less.[13] The provisions of employment standards legislation generally require a period of continuous employment with the same employer if a worker is to be eligible for vacations, longer vacations and statutory holidays or entitled to notice of dismissal, appeal of an unjust dismissal, and severance pay. Saskatchewan is unique in providing an annual vacation to workers with interrupted periods of employment with the same employer (if the periods are separated by no more than 182 days).

Saskatchewan is also alone in placing no limitations on the provision of statutory holidays — all workers are eligible. Of the seven jurisdictions providing for a longer vacation after extended periods of employment, only Manitoba and Saskatchewan allow the employment to be interrupted for certain periods, although it must still be with the same employer. All jurisdictions except the Northwest Territories have provisions for notice of dismissal for individual workers, but only two (New Brunswick and the Yukon) do not require a minimum period of employment.

Workers who leave and re-enter the labour force, or who are employed on a temporary basis, are likely to lose the minimum standards provided under the legislation. Separate periods of employment with the same employer rarely satisfy the eligibility requirements, while work with different employers is not provided for in any jurisdiction. Because women are employed in occupations characterized by less stability (such as service and sales work) and may experience interruptions in paid work as a result of family responsibilities, women are most likely to experience difficulty fulfilling the requirements of employment standards legislation that would entitle them to these benefits and protections.

Domestic Workers

Another group of workers often excluded from the protection of employment standards legislation is domestic workers. Although it is difficult to obtain accurate figures on the number of women employed as domestics, a recent publication by the Canadian Advisory Council on the Status of Women reports that in 1983, over 35,000 women came into Canada under temporary work permits. More than half these women were destined for service occupations, working primarily as live-in domestics in private Canadian homes.[14] The most complete statistics come from the Statistics Canada census data for 1981. In that year there were 28,120 women employed as housekeepers and servants and in related occupations in private households. Another 19,685 women were being paid to care for children in private households.[15] Although the latter figure includes self-employed women caring for children in their own homes (and therefore not subject to employment standards legislation), work in private households is not always reported. Consequently, the number of employed women caring for children is underestimated. With these caveats, it is reasonable to suggest that at least 48,000 women are employed as domestic workers. This work is done almost exclusively by women; just 665 men reported working in these occupations in 1981.

Domestic workers are excluded remarkably often from the provisions of employment standards legislation. In most jurisdictions domestic workers are not protected by provisions governing standard hours of work, are excluded from the right to receive overtime pay, and do not receive an annual vacation. In only five jurisdictions are all domestic workers entitled to statutory holidays. They are excluded from the right to notice of termination of employment in five of the jurisdictions that have such protection.

Only in Quebec are domestic workers covered by the same minimum wage rate as are other workers.[16] In Ontario and Manitoba, domestics working less than 24 hours per week are excluded from the minimum wage legislation, while in British Columbia and Newfoundland a special lower wage rate is set for domestics. Domestics caring for children in private homes are not eligible for the minimum wage in Prince Edward Island, and in Saskatchewan only employers receiving a publicly funded wage subsidy must pay the minimum wage rate to domestics. In the other six jurisdictions (domestic work is not covered under federal jurisdiction), domestics are excluded entirely from any wage protection under the legislation.

The legal rights of many domestic workers are more complex if they are not Canadian citizens and are working in this country on temporary employment visas. In 1984, Employment and Immigration Canada issued 15,323 such visas, although this is not the actual number of workers, because some workers would receive more than one visa during the year.[17] However, an unknown number of domestics work illegally in Canada and are not included in this figure.

Although domestic workers are often excluded from protection in employment standards legislation, the federal Canada Immigration Centres do require employers to guarantee some minimum rights to domestics on temporary work visas. The established pay and conditions vary from province to province. In Ontario, for which the greatest number of temporary work visas are issued, the required pay rate is $137.50 per week, over and above any amount payable for room and board, and the hours of work are set at 44 per week. As this translates to $4.37 per hour, the rate is actually higher than the provincial minimum wage rate of $4.00 an hour, and the hours of work are the same as those in the employment standards legislation. However, serious questions have been raised about the actual treatment of domestic workers on work visas and their conditions of employment.

In interviews with ten women from the English-speaking Caribbean (Jamaica, Trinidad, St. Vincent, Antigua, St. Lucia, and Guyana) on temporary work visas, Makeda Silvera found that their work situations commonly violated the regulations.[18] Most were alone in this country, cut off from their own cultures, and therefore largely dependent on the family

78

they worked for. Some domestics were lucky and found a family that treated them well. However, often employers took advantage of them by paying less than the contract, sometimes as little as $200.00 a month, requiring overtime with no pay, depriving them of their privacy, and in some cases inflicting verbal and physical abuse on them.

Silvera found that, often, the women were afraid to complain to Employment and Immigration Canada because if the complaint resulted in loss of their jobs, they had to find new employment or risk losing their visas. This put pressure on them to accept another potentially unsatisfactory situation, making them even more vulnerable. The women in this study put up with intolerable conditions because most of them were sending money back home to support their children. The threat of loss of income made these women vulnerable to exploitation. They were prepared to tolerate poor conditions rather than face losing their only chance of helping their own families.

Homeworkers

Information on people who work in their homes at piece rates is limited. Laura Johnson's book, *The Seam Allowance*, based on interviews with immigrant women doing industrial home-sewing on a piece-rate basis, provides some important insights into the wages and working conditions of homeworkers.[19] In her interviews, Johnson found most homeworkers to be immigrant women who had young children and worked for long hours sewing for piece rates while caring for their families. Many of the women were experienced seamstresses who had worked in factories before having children.

Despite their experience, homeworkers often made less than minimum wage. Johnson estimates that the average pay for a homeworker doing industrial sewing full-time over the period 1978 to 1980, was $4,136.00 a year — less than $100.00 per week. Another study cited a woman who packaged Shake and Bake in her home. She worked full days and, with her children's help, was able to make $45.00 a week in 1980.[20] Working in the home isolates women from co-workers, making it almost impossible for them to unionize to protest poor working conditions. The woman carries the burden of caring for her children and her home while doing industrial homework for long hours, low pay, and no benefits.

The majority of homeworkers are employed in Ontario and Quebec, where the bulk of manufacturing in Canada takes place. Homeworkers have some coverage under employment standards legislation in these two provinces. In Ontario, employers are required to pay homeworkers the equivalent of minimum wage and 4% holiday pay. However, homeworkers are specifically excluded from employment standards governing hours of work, overtime, and public holidays. Maternity leave, termination of employment, and employer benefit plans are rarely applicable. In 1980, Quebec revised its *Employment Standards Act* to guarantee homeworkers the same basic rights as other workers. In addition, homework in the women's garment industry in Quebec is covered by a ministerial decree. Employers are required to pay homeworkers rates 10% more than the factory rate, to pay when goods are picked up, and to provide thread and transportation; they are prohibited from charging the homeworker for the cost of redoing work.[21]

Johnson found that although both provinces offer some legislative protection for homeworkers, the laws go unenforced, as the majority of employers operate illegally without a permit. Based on a Toronto survey, she estimated that two-thirds of employers of homeworkers are operating illegally. Operating without a permit allows employers to avoid meeting legal requirements. Employers are not actively monitored by the government; instead, the employee must file a complaint against the employer. In some cases, they may fear losing their jobs; in other instances, they are illegal immigrants who fear deportation. By specifying investigations only of individual complaints, the law fails to recognize the lack of power these workers have in relation to their employers. The failure of governments to impose severe penalties and to monitor working conditions of homeworkers means that, in practice, most homework goes unregulated. Improving protection for homeworkers is particularly important in light of the potential to move computerized office work into the home as a way for employers to reduce overhead costs.

WHAT NEEDS TO CHANGE

Expand Legislative Coverage

As legislation intended to provide a basic standard of working conditions and pay, employment standards laws should apply to all workers. The exclusions prevalent in many provinces deprive those groups of workers of any protection in employment. However, on most issues, one or more jurisdictions have implemented improved coverage, indicating that it can indeed be done. As examples, in Quebec, domestic workers are covered by minimum wage legislation, and in Saskatchewan workers are not required to fulfil a period of employment to be eligible for statutory holidays.

Improve the Range of Rights and Benefits

The current standards in many provinces are not generous, especially compared to legislated provisions in European countries. New standards with respect to hours of work, overtime, and vacations are desirable and would contribute to reducing unemployment. No jurisdiction protects against loss of income because a worker is ill, an omission that should be rectified.

80

Increased minimum wage rates would improve the pay of many employed women. The rates need to be indexed to inflation so that their real value is not eroded by years without any increase.

The right of workers to appeal an unjust dismissal should be legislated in all jurisdictions, and without the severe restrictions in the three acts that now provide for appeal. This would provide increased job security for workers and the possibility of reinstatement where an appeal was upheld.

Strengthen Enforcement Mechanisms

A statutory means of pursuing workers' complaints should be made available for recovery of all outstanding compensation, without the limits that now exist in four provinces. This would enable a worker to use the faster and less costly method of obtaining unpaid debts from an employer, without having to take further action through the civil courts for amounts beyond the statutory minimums or established limits.

Where an amicable settlement cannot be arranged by an employment standards official and further action is necessary, the costs involved should not fall on the worker, since this discourages workers from pressing claims.

NOTES

1. Unpublished data provided by Labour Canada for October 1985.

2. Canada, Statistics Canada, *The Labour Force* (Ottawa: Supply and Services Canada, 1985), catalogue no. 71-001, table 79.

3. The Canadian Labour Congress supports a legislative ban on overtime.

4. Canada, Labour Canada, *Labour Standards in Canada*, 1984 edition (Ottawa: Supply and Services Canada, 1984), p. 58.

5. Canada, Statistics Canada, *The Labour Force*, table 74.

6. Dr. R. Blanpain, *International Encyclopedia for Labour Law and Industrial Relations* (Deventer, Netherlands: Kluwer Law and Taxation Publishers, 1985).

7. *Ibid*.

8. Calculated from unpublished data provided by Statistics Canada, Special Surveys Division, from the Survey of Union Membership, December 1984.

9. Lorraine Payette, "Et les oubliées du Code du Travail", *La vie en rose* (May 1985), pp. 32-34.

10. Canada, Statistics Canada, *The Labour Force*, table 82.

11. *Ibid*., table 83.

12. Canada, Labour Canada, *Part-Time Work in Canada*, report of the Commission of Inquiry into Part-Time Work (Ottawa: Supply and Services Canada, 1983), p. 29.

13. Canada, Statistics Canada, *The Labour Force*, table 74.

14. Alma Estable, *Immigrant Women in Canada: Current Issues* (Ottawa: Canadian Advisory Council on the Status of Women, 1986), p. 29.

15. Canada, Statistics Canada, *1981 Census of Population, Labour Force Industry by Occupation* (Ottawa: Supply and Services Canada, 1984), catalogue no. 92-923, table 2, p. 557.

16. This applies to live-out domestic workers; other arrangements are specified for domestic workers who live in their employers' homes.

17. Information provided by Employment and Immigration Canada.

18. Makeda Silvera, *Silenced* (Toronto: Williams-Wallace Publishers, 1983).

19. Laura C. Johnson, *The Seam Allowance: Industrial Home Sewing in Canada* (Toronto: The Women's Educational Press, 1982).

20. Francine Lepage and Anne Gauthier, *Syndicalisation : droit à acquérir, outil à conquérir : étude sur les travailleuses non syndiquées au Québec* (Quebec : Council on the status of women, 1981), p. 15.

21. Laura C. Johnson, *The Seam Allowance*, pp. 110-111. Under the *Act Respecting Collective Agreement Decrees*, either party can apply to the Minister of Labour and Manpower to pass a decree making a collective agreement binding on all employees in the industry. The decree is administered by a joint committee. These decrees have been established in the following industries: apparel, ladies clothing and suits, boys clothing, and gloves. They deal specifically with homework and vary with the industry.

CHAPTER SIX

OCCUPATIONAL HEALTH AND SAFETY

I became a VDT operator in 1976 and stuck it out for nearly three years. My job was to process information by typing on a computer terminal. The job demands that you sit still all day, staring at a screen which is about 25 inches from your face... It's potentially damaging to your health for several reasons. First, you are prevented from exercising most of your body, you can only leave your seat to go to the toilet. Where I worked we had no fresh air and the central heating was stifling. I suffered from continual colds and coughs... Our chairs were supposed to be adjustable, but most of them were broken and the firm didn't waste money mending them. Most women had backaches or neck cramps... The lighting was the florescent strip variety, which shone on the screen so that you couldn't see the print without turning up the brightness, and this really hurts your eyes after the first couple of hours... The print on the screen was lime green (this is the cheapest to buy) and it makes you feel sick... Having done this work for a few months, I realised that my eyesight was affected. When I left work I could hardly see across the road, although this used to wear off after a couple of hours. We all suffered with frequent headaches and carried aspirins around with us...[1]

The World Health Organization defines health as "a state of complete physical, mental, and social well-being and not merely the absence of disease and infirmity". Based on this definition, it is unlikely that many women workers would describe themselves as healthy, particularly considering the type of work they do and the environments in which they work.

The words occupational health and safety usually conjure up mental images of men in hard hats and heavy work boots — construction workers or miners — who are exposed to an array of well-known workplace hazards: high-voltage electrical wires, heavy machinery, vats of molten metal. Less publicized, but equally important, are the hazards associated with the places where most Canadian women work: in offices, banks, stores, restaurants, hospitals, medical laboratories, schools, child care centres, and hairdressing establishments.

It has been well documented that women in the paid labour force are largely segregated into a few occupational categories. Less recognized is the fact that, as a result of this segregated status, most women in the paid labour force are exposed to particular types of health and safety hazards associated with these ghettoized jobs. These hazards are all too familiar to the thousands of women who face them on a regular basis.[2]

Clerical workers — secretaries, typists, clerks, telephone operators, word processor operators — are frequently exposed to poor lighting, excessive noise, toxic substances, and poor ventilation. Many spend long hours sitting in poorly designed furniture, working in routine, monotonous jobs. Retail and service workers — sales clerks, cashiers, waitresses, bank tellers — face health and safety hazards associated with bending, lifting, and carrying. Many develop varicose veins and foot problems as a result of long hours of standing. Hairdressers working around tonics, dyes, pungent chemicals, and aerosol sprays on a daily basis are susceptible to respiratory problems and skin conditions. Teachers and child care workers are continually exposed to a variety of communicable diseases. So are nurses and other women in health-related fields. In addition, health care workers are susceptible to falls, back injuries, and needle punctures. Exposure to radiation, anaesthetic gases, and other toxic substances are additional hazards for hospital workers, dental assistants, and technicians.

In the last two decades, technological advancements in the workplace have opened the door for new health risks. The widespread introduction of video display terminals (VDTs) has produced new health-related problems and given rise to additional fears about safety at the workplace. Many women who spend large blocks of time working at these terminals suffer from eyestrain, headaches, back, neck, or wrist pain. They worry about exposure to radiation and suffer from increased stress. Another recently identified workplace hazard is sealed building syndrome, a problem arising in part from continued recirculation of pollutants because of insufficient air changes. Many women who work in poorly ventilated sealed buildings suffer from headaches, respiratory problems, and increased fatigue but have difficulty identifying any discernible source of the trouble.

The same hazards that threaten women in the paid work force may also prevail in the home environment, yet the home is not generally recognized as a workplace. As a result, potentially hazardous substances used regularly in homes are not identified, monitored or controlled, leaving women who work in the home largely unprotected. Toxic substances are found in many home cleaning products, including detergents, soaps, polishes, waxes, and removers. Some pesticides and insecticides commonly tracked in from the garden or used inside the house in the form of ant traps or pest strips also contain toxic substances.[3] These home products pose a threat to

86

the women who work full-time in the home, as well as to women who work both in the home and in the paid labour force.

For most women workers, regardless of their place of work, stress is a common problem. Numerous health problems have been associated with or aggravated by stress, such as headaches, fatigue, ulcers, asthma, insomnia, and coronary heart disease.[4] Many factors have been found to contribute to stress, including heavy workload, low pay, little job control, lack of recognition, monotonous work, and unrealistic deadlines.[5] In her article, "The Home is the Workplace",[6] Harriet Rosenberg documents other common sources of stress, such as lack of participation in decision making, low job satisfaction, no opportunity to learn new skills, too slow or too fast a pace, confinement to a work area, discrimination and rigid work roles, lack of job security, and abuse, noting that these sources of stress apply to those doing housework as well as those performing other types of work. A 1977 study conducted by the U.S. National Institute for Safety and Health found that secretaries had the second highest incidence of stress-related disease among workers in 130 occupations.[7] Not surprisingly, many women find that the multiple responsibilities of paid work, family care, and domestic work greatly increase their stress level.

The complexity of the health and safety issue is compounded by the fact that hazards are not always confined to areas that are traditionally defined as the workplace. For example, workers can carry home dusts and chemicals in their clothes and in their hair, inadvertently exposing their families to dangerous or potentially dangerous substances. On a broader scale, industrial waste in the water and in the air affects the health of whole communities.

One of the most alarming aspects of workplace hazards is their potential to cause genetic or reproductive damage. Occupational hazards affecting reproductive ability have a detrimental impact not only on pregnant females and developing fetuses, but also on males and non-pregnant females. Affected workers can suffer serious consequences, such as impaired sexual functioning, sterility, miscarriage, and offspring with physical defects.[8]

Workplace health and safety is an issue of increasing concern as more people become aware of its far-reaching implications. Workers who have been injured or become ill because of their work, risk short or long-term disability, reduced income, and loss of work. They suffer from reduced productivity, lowered morale, and loss of status and self-esteem. Many cannot continue in their present line of paid work, while family life and the ability to carry out domestic tasks may also be affected.

Employers are also aware of the issue and are designing policies and programs to address these concerns. These include providing fitness programs, developing preventive measures on smoking and cardiovascular disease, and designing programs to curb alcohol abuse.

THE LEGISLATION AND ITS PROBLEMS

Most workers in Canada are covered by legislation that offers some degree of protection against workplace health and safety hazards. The relevant statutes passed by legislatures spell out the rights and responsibilities of both workers and employers. Many acts are accompanied by regulations that detail more precisely the obligations, standards, and procedures outlined in the law. These regulations are as binding in law as the acts themselves. In addition, some workplaces are governed by guidelines and codes of practice that are set out by the employer and intended to provide a general framework for workplace health and safety. Such guidelines are usually not legally binding.

Complexity of the Legislation

Neither the federal government nor any of the provinces has enacted a single piece of legislation encompassing all aspects of workplace health and safety. Thus, there may be a general health and safety statute, or a number of laws that address workplace health and safety. In addition, there may be statutes governing certain sectors, such as mines or construction. Most jurisdictions also have hazard-oriented laws to cover areas such as pesticides, explosives, environmental contaminants, and fire hazards. Some workers may be affected by both the legislation that governs their workplace generally and the legislation relating to a particular hazard.

In addition to jurisdictional and legislative fragmentation, responsibility for administering and enforcing the laws is usually divided among several departments or agencies. Thus, for example, at the federal level alone, 13 different departments or agencies are involved in the administration and enforcement of 25 acts pertaining to occupational health and safety. Across Canada, there are 13 jurisdictions (federal, provincial, and territorial) with 108 different agencies administering and enforcing 241 different acts.[9] With such a complex labyrinth, many workers find it a real challenge to determine which acts and regulations apply to them. When they do, they must keep abreast of changes. The Ontario law, for example, was recently amended to include teachers and teaching assistants at universities. Nova Scotia has new occupational health and safety legislation, proclaimed on January 1, 1986.

Given the complex structure and administration of laws and regulations pertaining to workplace health and safety, the central question is this: What does this array of legislation provide? The simple answer: some protection for some workers.

The discussion that follows is intended to provide an overview of some legislative provisions, giving an indication of the type and scope of protection provided to workers through legislation. The provisions vary widely, however, not only from one jurisdiction to another, but also from workplace to workplace. Therefore, it is important for every worker to find out, first, whether she is covered by legislation; second, precisely what protection she has; and third, what other options are available to assist her in securing a workplace that is both healthy and safe.

Legislated Provisions

■   Duties of workers and employers

Generally speaking, under legislation, most employers have a duty to take reasonable care for the safety and health of their workers, to carry out procedures and techniques in a manner that prevents or reduces the risk of injury, and to provide notification to a designated authority if there is an accident, injury, or death. In addition, most jurisdictions impose a duty on employers to train workers adequately to handle safely the job they have been assigned.

The legislation usually directs workers to be responsible for taking reasonable care in protecting their own health and safety and that of their fellow workers, ensuring that they use protective devices where designated, operate equipment in a safe manner, and inform themselves of proper procedures.

■   Health and safety committees

One of the most effective means for workers to exercise some control over their workplace is through a worker-management health and safety committee. Legislative provision for such committees is relatively recent in this country (within the last two decades). The theory behind these committees is that a system that makes both labour and management internally responsible for health and safety is both more effective and less expensive than is one relying exclusively on the guardianship of the government.[10]

With the exception of Prince Edward Island, all jurisdictions have provisions in their legislation for joint labour-management health and safety committees. The provisions vary with respect to whether the committees are mandatory; the size of work force required (usually between 10 and 20 workers); and the size, composition, and role of the committee. Committees are usually empowered to receive complaints; maintain records of

89

complaints, accidents, and injuries; establish educational programs for workers; participate in inquiries and investigations regarding health and safety; examine reports related to the health and safety of the workers represented by the committee; request from the employer information considered necessary by the committee to identify hazards at the workplace; develop protective programs and procedures; and monitor existing programs and procedures related to workplace health and safety.

Organized labour generally takes the view that to do a proper job, committees need complete access to information, rigorous training, and sufficient authority to make some binding decisions about the workplace. Management sometimes questions the amount of information that committees really need and views them as advisory only. Government also views the committees as advisory, but will sometimes provide them with information, counselling, and training. One consequence of these various perspectives on the role of health and safety committees is that there are differences between the jurisdictions with respect to the support and authority given to these committees.[11]

Although many experts believe that the existence of health and safety committees has the potential to reduce the hazardous nature of some workplaces, there are recognized limitations to the provisions. In general, the committees, by law, exercise advisory powers only: they cannot legally bind management by their decisions, cannot close down an operation, and cannot stop management from introducing a potentially dangerous substance, machine or process.[12] However, in Quebec the committees do have some broader functions, including choosing the physician in charge of health services, approving the health program, and selecting individual protective devices.

Another problem is that the legislation is sometimes interpreted in such a way that although it is technically being followed, in practice the committees are not working as intended. For example, a 1983 examination of the Ontario occupational health and safety law by an NDP task force found that in some workplaces, management controlled the health and safety committees by influencing those areas not clearly defined in the act — calling and chairing meetings, setting the agenda, and keeping the minutes.[13] This clearly had a restraining effect inconsistent with the intent of establishing joint committees.

Perhaps the most serious limitation of the committees from the perspective of women workers is that some legislation permits the exclusion of some workplaces from the need to establish a committee. Alberta, Manitoba, and Newfoundland do not require committees in any workplace unless it is specified by regulation or by notice from the Minister of Labour. Other jurisdictions provide that committees must be established in workplaces with a minimum number of workers, usually 10 or 20. However, in Ontario, while committees are mandatory in workplaces with more than

20 workers, some workplaces are specifically exempted. Exempted workplaces include those where many women work, such as offices, shops providing goods or services to the public, apartment complexes, libraries, museums, art galleries, theatres, social organizations or clubs and, except for their kitchens and laundries, licensed restaurants, hotels, and motels. These provisions have serious implications for the many women workers who are specifically denied the protection that health and safety committees can offer.

■ Right to information

Workers are generally entitled to information about the health and safety of the workplace as well as to adequate instruction in the safe performance of their work. This type of information is essential so that workers can be aware of current or potential hazards in their workplaces. Health and safety committees are one of the best tools for providing information to workers. Where such committees exist, they should collect technical information for workers on products and processes used in the workplace; statistics on accidents and disease; results of testing and monitoring; inventories of chemical and biological agents currently used in the workplace; and information about products or procedures about to be introduced. If no committee exists, unionized workers should attempt to ensure access to information by negotiating specific contract language during collective bargaining. Non-unionized workers should exert pressure to ensure that comprehensive information is readily provided by the employer and understood by the workers.

■ Right to refuse work

Although the wording is different in the various acts, as a general rule most workers have a legislated right to refuse work that would endanger their health or safety. The notable exception is workers who fall under provincial legislation in Prince Edward Island.

The provisions are intended to ensure that if performing a job imperils a worker or co-worker's health and safety, a worker cannot be disciplined for refusing to do the job. In Quebec, this right may not be exercised if it puts another person in immediate danger or if the conditions of work are ordinary for the particular kind of work involved. In Ontario, police officers, fire fighters, and workers in correctional institutions may not refuse. Other workers in Ontario — those in health care facilities, group homes, ambulance services, laundries, food services, or power plants — can refuse only when doing so does not jeopardize the life, health, or safety of another person.

The right to refuse provision is also limited by the varying technical interpretations of the language in the legislation. In Alberta, there must be "imminent" danger; in British Columbia, there has to be an "undue" hazard present. In provinces where the legislation says the worker can refuse work when she has "reason to believe" a hazard exists, there may be variations in how "reason to believe" is interpreted.

Sometimes refusal to work by one worker affects others in the workplace. For example, if a woman on an assembly line refuses to work because of what she believes to be a hazardous situation, the whole assembly line may have to be shut down until a solution is reached. In the meantime, payment of the workers is not always guaranteed. This can lead to resentment and subtle pressure; only in Quebec does the legislation provide against loss of pay for workers whose jobs are halted because of someone's refusal to work.[14]

■ Control of toxic substances

Several jurisdictions have legislation to control the introduction and use of toxic substances in the workplace. Common features addressed by legislation include inventory control, testing, priority and standard setting, exposure limits, and mandatory procedures associated with these limits. However, there is no uniformity in terminology, even in terms of what constitutes a toxic substance.

Where they exist, health and safety committees can obtain information about toxic substances that exist in their workplaces and can share this information with workers. Some unions have negotiated collective agreements requiring that the union be given data sheets on all chemicals used in the workplace.[15] In other situations, workers should ask the employer to provide information on toxic substances used in the workplace.

Amendments to federal legislation, tabled in June 1987, would greatly enhance workers' access to information by establishing a Workplace Hazardous Materials Information System (WHMIS). WHMIS would require material safety data sheets, labelling, and training of workers where hazardous substances are used. It is intended that this system be used by the provinces as well.

The basic information that should be available to workers about toxic substances includes which ones are used in the particular workplace, the purpose of each, how they are used, what contact workers have with these substances, the known health effects, whether the effect of the substances could increase the risk of accidents, and whether two or more substances acting together could produce a magnified effect. Workers should also know whether an exposure limit has been set, whether there are any special conditions under which the substance could generate toxic products, and what control methods are recommended, available, and in use.[16]

In most provinces, standards are based upon those set by the American Conference of Governmental Industrial Hygienists (ACGIH), a private group in the United States. This organization establishes time-weighted measures as guidelines for acceptable levels of exposure to toxic substances; the measures are called Threshold Limit Values (TLVs). It is believed that most workers can be exposed repeatedly on a daily basis to the TLVs without adverse effects. However, there are several drawbacks associated with the use of TLVs, and many experts believe that they should not be used to determine what is and what is not a safe exposure level.

TLVs have been established for about 600 substances, but there are thousands of workplace substances for which no TLV has been set. It has been estimated that as many as 15,000 substances are in common use in industry, and that many times this number are used when all workplaces are taken into account.[17] In addition, TLVs are often used as if only one substance were present, but it is rare to find a workplace where only one substance exists. Their effects when substances are combined are virtually unknown.

The system of exposure limits established by the ACGIH and used in Canada differs from those set up in other countries. Where disparities exist, which system is safer? For example, some TLVs may be set too high. In the past, standards for asbestos were based upon studies that did not show that asbestos can cause cancer. The standards have been changed, but some workers already had cancer, and it is not known whether the new standards are in fact low enough to protect workers exposed to asbestos.

The ACGIH accepts that the TLVs they have established will not protect all workers all the time; they are intended only as guidelines. However, in Canada, those TLVs are frequently referred to in legislation and thus take on the force of law. As a result, a standard intended to be a guideline often becomes the rule for determining what is safe.

■ Prohibition of reprisals

Ideally, workers should be protected against reprisals for participating in any legitimate health and safety activity. However, the legislative protection against reprisals is very uneven. In the Yukon and Prince Edward Island, there is no legislated protection at all. Most provincial legislation addresses the issue by listing specific activities that are protected against reprisals, such as exercising the right to refuse dangerous work, or participating on a joint health and safety committee. Most of these lists are not comprehensive. Ontario's legislation appears to provide the best protection, since it protects workers from employer reprisals if the worker has acted in compliance with the act or its regulations.

Workers may find that it is often difficult to prove that a specific action constitutes a reprisal. Employers may not take official action, such as a reprimand or a discharge, to punish a worker, but may resort to more subtle forms of harassment, such as reassigning a worker with a health and safety complaint to a menial or unpleasant job. In his book, *Canadian Occupational Health and Safety Law*, Michael Nash points out that the "difficult cases involve situations where the employee acted out of an apparently legitimate concern for health and safety, but because of other factors in his or her work history, was fired or disciplined anyway."[18] Nash relates a case where a labour relations board found that an employee had proper grounds for a complaint about inadequate heating, but her complaint to the board against her firing was dismissed because the employer was found justified in firing her for the insubordination she displayed in voicing her complaint and in subsequently threatening her employer.

■ Enforcement provisions

Most jurisdictions address enforcement of the legislation by outlining the duties, rights, and responsibilities of inspection officers, and by detailing the offences and penalties for non-compliance with the act. The legislation governing occupational health and safety is generally based on the premise that the majority of people to whom it applies will voluntarily comply with the responsibilities imposed on them and with the minimum standards set forth. Inspectors have the responsibility to ensure that the law is upheld.

Many areas of jurisdiction, however, do not have sufficient numbers of inspectors to ensure compliance. As one researcher commented,

> the average number of companies and employees per inspector is high compared with the time and resources necessary to effectively audit environmental and behavioural hazards in the workplace...the inspectors have been forced to reduce the time they spend on individual inspections in favour of increasing the frequency of these inspections across a range of workplaces. And as a result, the inspectors often feel that they end up playing the role of safety co-ordinator for individual companies who wait until the inspector shows up before correcting hazards in their operation.[19]

Where voluntary compliance does not work, stop-work orders and prosecutions with fines and/or imprisonment are the two major instruments of enforcement. However, when inspectors issue orders to clean up a workplace, they are not always followed. For example, between 1979 and 1983, a firm in Windsor, Ontario, was ordered 29 times to clean up dust in the workplace. The issue was given press coverage after the order was consistently ignored by the employer and a worker had contracted a disease associated with the dust.[20]

When employers are prosecuted, the conviction rate is very low. In addition, the fines, when levied, are often so paltry that they fail to serve as an effective deterrent. In Alberta, the maximum fine is $15,000, but the average fine per conviction in 1983 was $1,533.[21]

■   Exemptions

Despite recognized weaknesses in laws and their enforcement, some workers do not get even the limited protection afforded by the legislation. Most legislation includes workers falling under the jurisdiction of the relevant legislatures. Many provinces, however, have specific exceptions. Domestic workers, farm workers, and casual workers are specifically excluded in some provinces. Municipal workers are excluded in Prince Edward Island. The effect of these exclusionary provisions is that many women workers across the country work in places that are not protected by legislation.

In summary, the regulatory approach to occupational health and safety has several inherent weaknesses. There are no minimum national standards governing health and safety in the workplace; instead, provisions vary across the thirteen jurisdictions. The legislation pertaining to health and safety is a confusing maze of acts, regulations, and standards. Jurisdiction is fragmented not only between federal, provincial, and territorial governments, but also among several departments at each level. The presence of legislation can give workers a false sense of security, since it may be poorly monitored and enforced. In many cases, the wording is ambiguous and does not afford workers the level of protection they may think they have. Many workers, particularly women workers, are not covered, even where legislation does exist. One area of particular weakness in legislation is that of protection against reproductive hazards in the workplace.

REPRODUCTIVE HAZARDS

Many hazards in the workplace may damage the reproductive capacity of a worker, cause genetic damage, or harm a fetus. Some of these hazards have been identified, others are suspected, and the effects of still others are as yet unknown. The implications of reproductive hazards are profound, because not only the health of workers is at stake, but also that of future generations.

Hazards that affect the reproductive system are not always immediately apparent, and the nature of the cause and effect relationship is not always clear. Lead, for example, causes nervous disorders, blood disease, and birth defects. However, it has also been shown to cause sterility in men and spontaneous abortions in the wives of male workers exposed to it.[22] Nurses in operating rooms who are exposed to anaesthetic gases also have a high rate of miscarriages.

Some employers have responded to reproductive hazards by excluding pregnant women, or all women of childbearing age, from certain workplaces. One reason for this practice is that an employer can be sued if a birth defect or deformity is proved to have been caused by exposure to a hazard in the workplace. Alternatives to excluding these workers include implementing appropriate and effective engineering controls or substituting safer substances. However, since this can be costly, some employers in Canada — such as Inco Metals, General Motors of Canada, Ontario Hydro, and Hudson Bay Mining and Smelting — have banned fertile women from certain jobs.[23] This has happened in predominantly male-dominated workplaces, such as smelting operations, battery plants, and other workplaces with known hazards, including vinyl chloride, lead, or radiation. As a result, some women have resorted to sterilization in order to maintain employment.

Excluding women from certain jobs on the grounds of potential reproductive damage is a specious policy, for several reasons. First, it presumes that all fertile women will become pregnant. Second, it reflects a double standard by implying that reproductive hazards are serious enough to warrant exclusion of fertile women from only some specific workplaces. In many areas where women traditionally work, reproductive threats are clearly recognized, but there has been no move by employers to ban women from them. Nursing and teaching, for example, present identified occupational hazards, but there has been no attempt to exclude fertile women from hospitals or schools or from other workplaces where women traditionally work, such as dry cleaning or hairdressing establishments. The exclusionary approach further ignores the fact that the reproductive ability of men can also be affected by workplace hazards. There is convincing documentation that a wide variety of substances can cause infertility and impotence in men. Finally, exclusion policies focus the burden of health and safety on the worker, instead of on the owner and manager of the workplace.

The legislative route has offered extremely limited protection. In Quebec, the *Occupational Health and Safety Act* of 1979 provides for the right of pregnant and nursing mothers to be assigned away from work areas that pose a physical danger. If a safe job is not available, the worker can take a leave of absence and receive worker's compensation. This legislation is unique in Canada. Although progressive, the legislation does have some drawbacks. It ignores the possibility of genetic damage. It cannot guarantee that no fetal damage will occur before a women knows she is pregnant. Moreover, it does nothing to protect the rest of the work force exposed to the same hazard; it removes the pregnant or nursing workers rather than reducing or eliminating the workplace hazard for the protection of all workers.

Women are pursuing other options in the hope of obtaining protection from reproductive hazards in the workplace. Human rights, labour relations, and legal systems are being used to challenge employer policies on reproductive hazards. At the time of writing, there was a complaint before the Canadian Human Rights Commission from a group of employees at Hudson Bay Mining and Smelting in Manitoba. They contended that the company discriminates against both men and women by excluding women from high lead exposure areas, at the same time subjecting men to elevated risk. In addition, a precedent may be set by a worker who is suing her former employer on behalf of her child, whose birth defects she believes were caused by overexposure to chemicals during early pregnancy.[24]

Collective bargaining is another instrument that has been used effectively to improve protection against reproductive damage. This has been particularly true in the case of pregnant workers who have the negotiated right to be transferred away from working around VDTs during pregnancy.

Some have suggested that the Canadian Charter of Rights and Freedoms may be used to challenge discriminatory policies arising from reproductive hazards in the workplace. Others have explored using the legislated right to refuse unsafe work.

It is clear that the ultimate goal is a workplace where the health of all workers and of future generations is ensured. However, achievement of this goal may be a long time coming. Not all reproductive hazards have been identified, the process of setting standards for known hazards is slow, and the hazards are numerous. Employers may hesitate to initiate action that might be costly. Given these difficulties, it has been acknowledged reluctantly that, in some circumstances, the next best alternative may be to remove susceptible workers from exposure to reproductive hazards. As Marianne Langton points out, however, "deciding on the terms of such removal often involves steering a tortuous course between the demands of job equity and those of reproductive health."[25] Langton outlines several factors that should be considered if this route is followed, among them defining susceptible workers, compensating workers who are removed or excluded from certain jobs, assessing the risk posed by the hazard in question, and ensuring the right of workers to exercise choice with respect to their reproductive and work lives. Weighing these factors is not easy. One option proposed is the removal or exclusion of a worker from a job during periods of temporary reproductive sensitivity, which would include pregnancy, lactation, or periods when conception is being attempted.[26]

Although transfers or removals are an option, clearly such measures should be considered temporary safeguards and not effective solutions. Workers must continue to press for healthy workplaces. The choice currently offered to some workers, predominantly women — choosing between a job and the right to reproduce — is unacceptable.

CONCLUSION

It is clear that existing legislation to protect workers from occupational health and safety hazards is inadequate. Not all workers are covered, the amount and extent of protection varies greatly from one jurisdiction to another, legislation that is in place is not always well monitored or enforced, and redress for non-compliance is weak or ineffective. More to the point, the legislation does not really address the hazards of workplaces where most women work. Notably absent are statutes and regulations governing poorly designed work stations, fumes from duplicating machines, sealed office buildings with poor ventilation, anaesthetic gases, viruses, noisy machines, stress, and many other debilitating hazards facing women workers daily.

Legislative change is necessary, but women also need to explore other options to ensure a healthier and safer work environment. This includes all women workers, whether they work in the paid work force, in the home, or both.

Women who are unionized have access to the collective bargaining process to initiate and implement improvements over and above legislated provisions. Legislation provides only minimum standards of protection to workers, and collective bargaining can be used to improve on these basic requirements and draw attention to new areas where action is needed. Where health and safety committees are not required by legislation, their establishment can be an item for negotiation. These committees have the potential to effect important changes at the workplace by educating workers, monitoring workplace environments, and insisting on improvements. Health and safety at the bargaining table is taking high priority, as workers become increasingly aware of the array of health and safety risks in their workplaces. Some unions have recently claimed victories by successfully negotiating improved working conditions for VDT operators, including specified rest breaks, eye protection, and leaves of absence for pregnant workers, as well as regular inspection and maintenance of the machines.

Compared to their non-unionized counterparts, unionized workers have much better health and safety protection, through collective agreements and through avenues such as appeals and grievance procedures. However, non-unionized women, including those who work in the home, can form organizations outside trade unions to deal with health and safety

98

issues. In some cities, such groups have organized to share information and publicize work-related problems. The Windsor Occupational Safety and Health group (WOSH) is one example. Women's Action on Occupational Health in Vancouver is another. In the United States, the Women's Occupational Health Resource Center has become a well known and highly respected source of information. The group conducts surveys of occupational environments and problem areas, circulates a regular newsletter, monitors legislation, provides informed speakers, and lobbies for change.

In order to effect change, women must educate themselves about their workplaces, the products and processes used, the hazards to which they (and their families) are exposed, and the legislative protection available. Forming or joining health and safety committees or groups is one method of doing this. Workers cannot rely on government to ensure healthy workplaces. In the absence of adequate laws, workers themselves have to press for improvements to obtain a safe and healthy working environment for everyone.

NOTES

1. Extract of a letter to *Women's Voice* (December 1979), quoted in Marianne Craig, *Office Workers' Survival Handbook: A Guide to Fighting Health Hazards in the Office*, British Society for Social Responsibility in Science (London: BSSRS Publications, 1981), p. 125.

2. For an excellent reference on occupational health hazards for women, see Jeanne Stellman, *Women's Work, Women's Health: Myths and Realities* (New York: Pantheon Books, 1977).

3. Harriet Rosenberg, "The Home Is the Workplace", in *Double Exposure: Women's Health Hazards on the Job and at Home*, ed. Wendy Chavkin (New York: Monthly Review Foundation, 1984), pp. 229-234.

4. Windsor Occupational Safety and Health Council, *A Worker's Guide to Health and Safety*, ed. Cecilia Deck, John Jackson and Hawley Shields (Toronto: 1982), p. 47.

5. Jeanne Stellman, *Women's Work*, pp. 54-80.

6. Harriet Rosenberg, "The Home Is the Workplace", pp. 223-227.

7. *National Safety News* (January 1979).

8. Nancy Miller Chenier, *Reproductive Health Hazards at Work* (Ottawa: Canadian Advisory Council on the Status of Women, 1982), p. 4.

9. Canadian Centre for Occupational Health and Safety, *A Mosaic of Mosaics: A Report on Occupational Health and Safety in Canada* (Don Mills, Ont.: CCH Canadian, 1983), p. 17.

10. Michael Izumi Nash, *Canadian Occupational Health and Safety Law Handbook* (Don Mills, Ont.: CCH Canadian, 1983), p. 59.

11. *Ibid.*, p. 60.

12. *Ibid.*, p. 74.

13. Ontario New Democratic Party Task Force on Occupational Health and Safety, *Not Yet Healthy, Not Yet Safe* (Toronto: 1983), p. 5.

14. Michael Izumi Nash, *Law Handbook*, p. 116.

15. Ontario Federation of Labour, *Occupational Health and Safety: A Training Manual* (Toronto, 1982), p. 63.

16. *Ibid.*, pp. 54-60.

17. *Ibid.*, p. 65.

18. Michael Izumi Nash, *Law Handbook*, pp. 163-164.

19. Hushion, Ogilvie Associates Limited, *An Assessment of the Effectiveness of Government Decision-Making Processes in the Field of Occupational Health and Safety*, Technical Report no. 5 (Ottawa: Economic Council of Canada, 1981), pp. 34-35.

20. "Firm Told 29 Times to Clean Up Dangerous Dust", *Toronto Star*, January 24, 1985.

21. Alberta, Occupational Health and Safety Division.

22. Ontario Federation of Labour, *Occupational Reproductive Hazards* (Toronto: n.d.), p. 11.

23. Marianne Langton, "Is Your Job Hazardous to Your Health?", in *Still Ain't Satisfied: Canadian Feminism Today*, ed. Maureen Fitzgerald, Connie Guberman, and Margie Wolfe (Toronto: The Women's Educational Press, 1982), p. 183.

24. "Lawsuit Against Factory Unique in Canada", *Canadian Occupational Health and Safety News*, vol. 7, no. 50 (December 17, 1984), p. 1. Cited in Marianne Langton, "Protecting Workers from Reproductive Hazards", presentation to the National Association of Women and the Law Biennial Conference, February 1985, p. 3.

25. Marianne Langton, "Protecting Workers from Reproductive Hazards", p. 5.

26. *Ibid.*, p. 7.

CHAPTER SEVEN

WOMEN AND UNIONS

Canadian working women have not been well represented in the ranks of organized labour. Many of the negative attitudes concerning women's participation in the paid labour force that were prevalent in the past no longer exist. Even so, women still face many obstacles, from both employers and co-workers, to their participation as equals within the trade union movement.

In the last 25 years, the female labour force has grown by 175%, from just under two million to five million. In contrast, the male labour force grew by only 45%. The growth in women's labour force participation was accompanied by a substantial increase in their union membership: a 300% increase for women, compared to a 65% increase in male membership. The increased unionization of women was more than just a function of their increased labour participation. Since the early 1970s the growth in women's unionization has exceeded the increase in their labour force participation by 12%; the unionization of men lags behind, by 12%.[1]

Despite this substantial rise, women still represent only 38.5% of total union membership.[2] Table 7.1 shows the degree of unionization for male and female workers in Canada.

Table 7.1   Union Membership and Collective Agreement Coverage
of Employed Paid Workers in Canada

	Female	Male	Total
% of Paid Labour Force	42.2	57.8	100
% Unionized	31.9	41.4	37.2
% Covered by a Collective Agreement	36.6	46.0	41.8
% of Total Union Membership	38.5	61.5	100

Source: Statistics Canada, unpublished data from the Survey of Union Membership, a supplement to *Labour Force Survey*, December 1984.

Neither women's rapid integration into paid work nor their political struggles of the past few decades have altered substantially their inequality in the labour force. Based on a recent assessment, men receive higher average incomes "for every occupational group, for every age group, for part-time and full-time workers, for every educational level and in every region in Canada."[3]

This chapter addresses historical, social and economic reasons for low union participation by Canadian women. It also explores some more fundamental questions. Does it matter to women's economic position that they are under-represented in unions? Do unions adequately address the needs and concerns of working women? Are unions more of a problem than a solution in working women's struggle for equality in the labour force?

THE EARLY YEARS

Unfortunately, Canadian historical studies of women workers are rare. Since Jean Scott published her pioneering investigation of Toronto women workers in 1891, there have been few academic studies of women workers, and even fewer of women in the Canadian trade union movement.[4] This neglect is primarily because women have formed a significantly smaller proportion of the unionized work force than men have done. Also, there are fewer sources available for research into women's labour history. Traditional labour sources — trade union and labour council records, the labour press, and government documents — are limited in their usefulness for women's history.[5]

However, to study women unionizing or in unions is to examine only a fraction of working women's experiences. It restricts us to the context of an organized and "male" labour history. Studies of women in trade unions must include the broader experience of working life, for women's trade union experiences are inseparable from their class, ethnic and family lives.[6]

We can begin to grasp the problem women have faced by looking at their working conditions in the late nineteenth and early twentieth centuries. In 1871, women and children made up over 50% of the work force in light manufacturing (shoemaking, printing, tobacco).[7] Almost universally, women's working conditions were worse than those for men, and women rarely earned enough to be self-sufficient; their wages were usually below the minimum living wage. For example, in 1913, the average female factory worker earned $4.50 to $5.50 per week, but the minimum living wage was estimated to be $7.00 per week.[8] Unskilled female workers received much lower wages than unskilled male workers did, apparently without any shame on the part of their employers, as a manufacturer of ready-made clothing indicated in an 1897 newspaper report:

I don't treat the men bad, but I even up by taking
advantage of the women. I have a girl who can do as
much work, and as good work as a man; she gets $5.00
a week. The man standing next to her gets $11.00. The
girls, however, average $3.50 a week, and some are as
low as $2.90.[9]

The only protest that women could make against harsh working
conditions and low pay was to vote with their feet by moving from job to
job. This might have relieved the monotony, but it did little to alleviate the
working conditions.

Despite inequitable pay rates, women failed to unionize in
significant numbers because of the fragmented and isolated nature of their
employment situations. The Royal Commission of 1896 to investigate the
"Sweating System in Canada" revealed that the greatest proportion of
women's paid labour was done at home, where factory laws were not
applicable and where women had little contact with other workers.
Fragmentation was also the norm for domestics, clerical workers and shop
girls, presenting a formidable barrier to any organizing attempt.[10]

Because women were almost always unskilled workers, employers
could replace them easily in the event of a strike. In that era, there was a
ready supply of workers, especially immigrants, willing to work for almost
any wage. In addition, the 1889 report of the Royal Commission on the
Relations of Labour and Capital gave evidence that employers strenuously
resisted women's attempts to organize.[11] Even where women worked
alongside men as a regular part of the work force, and where they had the
opportunity to join the unions organized by men, evidence indicates that
they were more subject to employer intimidation. There is even testimony
that, in some cases, women joining a union were automatically fired.

Women's occupations at the time also hindered union
organization. By the turn of the century, 41% of women in the labour force
were employed as domestics. The census of 1891 gave the leading
occupations of women as servants, dressmakers and seamstresses, all
traditional homemaker-type occupations. These jobs isolated women workers
from each other.[12] In these jobs, women were closely supervised, had very
little time off, and usually required little previous working experience. Most
of the women workers in this period were young and single because, for
most women, marriage marked their exit from the world of paid labour. As
is the case today, married women who did work for wages were burdened
with additional household responsibilities. Normally, they had little time or
energy for active participation in union or strike activities. Those few
married women who did work outside the home often moved in and out of
the paid labour force because of pregnancy.

Craft unions — the first strong unions to exist in the late nineteenth and early twentieth century — generally resisted admitting women to their ranks. The purpose of these associations of skilled workers was to maintain high standards of workmanship and to limit membership in order to keep the demand for their services relatively high. Women did not have an equal opportunity to learn labour skills, and because of the transitory nature of women's working lives, journeymen were not interested in taking them on as apprentices. To them, women were the cheap, unskilled labourers used to undercut their market.

For all these reasons — transience, lack of skills, lack of experience in the workplace, the extra demands of household responsibilities, isolation on the job, and employer opposition — women commonly faced insurmountable barriers to their participation in union activity. For male workers, active participation in the trade union movement required time, energy and dedication that were often extraordinary. For female workers, this effort was usually impossible.[13]

Early Attitudes to Working Women

By 1921, 20% of women over 14 years of age worked outside the home. Even so, the following comments appeared in the 1922 Annual Report of the Quebec Department of Labour:

> A woman's work, outside of her home, is one of the sad novelties of the modern world; it is a true social heresy... Such singularities are due to a fleeting crisis, the social crisis of present day... With regard to the work of a single woman, it would be wonderful if society could, some day or another, find an economic formula capable of doing away with it.[14]

In Canada, Victorian ideology defined women as inferior to men, fragile, emotional and in need of protection. The womanly ideal combined religious piety, moral purity and a complete commitment to domesticity. A women's only necessary role was as a wife and mother.

Clearly, working women contradicted this ideology and, as a result, provoked much concern and discussion. Middle-class women's organizations, reformers, factory inspectors and male labourers alike perceived working women as a "social crisis", creating problems of cleanliness, morality and health for future mothers.[15]

The union movement also viewed the primary role of women as a domestic one. Women's pages in labour publications bore articles about the wives and mothers of trade unionists and provided recipes and fashion discussions. A 1907 article entitled "The Influence of Women in the Labour

Movement" dealt exclusively with the role of women as consumers, wives and mothers. There was not a single reference to women in the workplace or in a union.[16]

Indeed, some of the most extreme opposition to women's organizing came from within the trade union movement. For professed humanitarian reasons, union leaders wanted to relieve women workers of the hardships of industrial life, rather than attempt to better women's working conditions and wages. Exclusion of women from the labour force was advocated actively. The Trades and Labour Congress of Canada, as part of its 16-point program in 1898, called for

> ...abolition of child labour by children under 14 years of age and female labour in all branches of industrial life, such as mines, workshops, factories, etc.[17]

Male unionists were usually of the opinion that women in the work force "had a tendency to lower the wages of men and to keep a number of young men out of work."[18] In 1904, Montreal bookbinders led a strike to force employers to fire women. The same union bargained in 1907 for lower increases for already poorly paid women workers. Male bookbinders were to earn $13.50 to $14.50 a week, while female bookbinders were to get $5.00 to $5.50 a week.[19]

Despite predominant attitudes, women workers gradually made advances in the union movement. Even while advocating exclusion of women from the labour force, the union movement also began to support unionization for those women who did continue to work. By 1914, the Trades and Labour Congress of Canada replaced its call for exclusion with a call for "equal pay for equal work for men and women."[20] In specific instances, the union movement, local unions or groups of male unionists supported women's rights as workers. For example, during the Toronto Bell Telephone strike in 1907, porters refused to work when strike breakers stayed in their hotel. In 1912, a strike by women boot and shoe workers over a pay reduction was endorsed and publicized by the union and supported by the men, who walked out in solidarity.[21]

World War I brought more women into the labour force and reduced opposition to working women. However, this increase in labour force participation was viewed as only a temporary aberration that would be remedied with the return of the soldiers.

Until the 1940s, the federal government advocated substitution of domestic labour for paid labour.[22] Suggested solutions to the "post-war problems of women" included family allowances (payable to women) and domestic training programs.

Economic and Labour Force Trends After World War II

World War II marked the end of the Great Depression and the beginning of "the longest uninterrupted boom the capitalist world economy has ever experienced."[23] It also marked an about-face in the government's extreme pre-war laissez-faire policy. The 1945 White Paper on Employment and Income indicated that the government would now be responsible for manipulating levels of aggregate demand to maintain "a high and stable level of employment and income."[24] Stabilization policies, medical care plans, pensions and other programs meant a dramatic increase in state spending. Between 1951 and 1971, governments' expenditures increased by a factor of four, to more than a third of the GNP. The state also became a major employer. By 1971, federal, provincial and municipal governments employed more than a million people.[25]

This restructuring of the economy saw a decline in the male-dominated agricultural sector and expansion of the service, finance and trade industries, where women were more likely to be employed. In terms of jobs, the primary sector declined absolutely as well as relatively between 1951 and 1971, the secondary sector more or less held its own in relative terms, and the tertiary sector expanded enormously. Demand for workers in traditionally female areas and in low-wage industries grew, while the number of jobs in sectors where males usually found work increased more slowly or even decreased.[26]

New products, new appliances and new services changed the structure of domestic labour as well, making it both necessary and easier in some cases for women to join the labour force. Extra income was needed to purchase these new items, and the time they saved meant that women could hold a job while maintaining a home. A woman's income, however, was still considered supplemental to the income of the "real breadwinner" — the husband.

Married women searching for paid employment competed for work in the trade and service sectors, where jobs were being created and where training periods and skill requirements were minimal. Women's wages remained low because large reserves of women workers were available and the simplification of tasks made workers easily replaceable. The restrictions imposed by household and family responsibilities still ensured that few female workers became involved in union activities. These conditions were reflected in the characteristics of the jobs women held in the trade and service industries: part-time and seasonal work and high turnover rates.

Between 1951 and 1971, "jobs also grew rapidly in the finance, insurance and real estate industries. Still, unionization and women's wages remained low."[27] Thus, although there was not much of an increase in employment in manufacturing, trade union membership in the financial sector increased substantially. As late as 1980, however, women made up

108

only 26% of the work force and 19% of union membership in the manufacturing sector.[28]

A large number of the women working in the food and clothing industries were organized. However, these unions were weakened by the part-time and seasonal nature of the work, by the size and relative strength of companies, by the large reserve female labour force, and by competition from imported products.[29]

Before the 1960s, there was little unionization of employees in the public sector. After this period, however, attitudes began to change, and trade unionism became more attractive to public servants. New white collar jobs and the passing of the *Public Service Staff Relations Act* in 1967 accounted for the growth in female public sector unionization in the 1970s.

By 1974, women represented 31.6% of the labour force, but only 22.7% of them were organized, representing 25.2% of total union membership in Canada.

CURRENT TRENDS AND ISSUES

Women now represent over 50% of the paid labour force; 31.9% are unionized, and this represents 38.5% of total union membership.[30] Women have organized at a much faster rate than have men in the last two decades (Table 7.2). The gap has narrowed rapidly since the 1960s, but women are still significantly less unionized than men.

Table 7.2   Unionization of Women in Canada, 1965-1984

	Number of Women Members	Percentage of All Members
1965	292,056	16.6
1970	513,203	22.6
1975	711,102	26.0
1979	890,365	29.3
1980	932,883	30.2
1984	1,336,200	38.5*

Source: (*) Pradeep Kumar and Mary Lou Coates, *The Current Industrial Relations Scene in Canada: 1986* (Kingston: Industrial Relations Centre, 1986); other data from L. Brisken and L. Yantz, ed., *Union Sisters: Women in the Labour Movement* (Toronto: The Women's Educational Press, 1983).

Why is it that all industries where women represent a third or more of the labour force (except public adminstration) have a lower degree of unionization than the industrial average?[31] The historical record is inconclusive about whether attitudes, on the part of women toward unions or of men toward organizing women, affect women's rates of unionization. On the other hand, the best contemporary evidence — based on what people do, not what they say — is quite clear. If social attitudes are the main barrier to female unionization, women should have a lower degree of unionization than men in the same industries. In Julie White's 1980 study, *Women and Unions*, the conclusion is clear that industry and occupation, not sex directly, are the variables to investigate in order to understand degrees of unionization.[32]

White's findings are reinforced by Briskin and Yantz in their 1983 study, *Union Sisters: Women in the Labour Movement*. Briskin and Yantz also state that the sector of the economy has a greater effect on unionization rates than the sex of the worker; they conclude that the trade union movement must look to those sectors with low rates of unionization in order to increase the numbers of unionized women.[33]

Analysis shows that two sectors with a very low degree of unionization employ large numbers of women. In finance, 358,000 women are employed (mostly by banks), while only 2.6% of them are unionized. Trade employs 746,000 women, but only 7.2% of them are unionized. Even in the service sector, where 25.3% of women workers are unionized, close to 1.3 million women workers are not unionized.[34]

Why are women employed in industries and occupations that have been poorly organized historically and where resistance to unionization remains? The answer lies in both the history of trade union organization and the opposition of employers. In general, less than 10% of workers were able to organize stable unions in the period before industrial unions emerged in the late 1930s.[35] The major unions that did exist were concentrated where women had sparse representation: the construction, mining, metal and railway trades.

During World War II, the necessities of the wartime economy gave labour increased leverage. Even then, however, acceptance of unionism did not extend to services such as clerical and financial work and public administration. As employment levelled off in the industrial sector after the post-war boom, union membership stagnated. Although changes in attitudes and in legislation affecting public employees eventually occurred in 1967 with the passage of the *Public Service Staff Relations Act*, no such change has yet occurred in the finance, trade and retail parts of the private sector.

At present, employer opposition and the large reserve of unemployed labour in sectors employing large numbers of women remain important factors in explaining the low degree of unionization among women.

The best example of concerted employer opposition is in the banking industry. In the mid-1970s, 75% of all workers employed by banks were women. Union statistics show that less than 1% of bank workers were unionized.[36] The Canada Labour Relations Board provides statistics showing banks have had more complaints laid against them than all the other industrial sectors it deals with. Labour Code violations have included firing staff for union activities, transferring workers involved in a union at one branch to a different branch, denying promotions to unionized employees, hiring additional workers at a branch in the process of unionizing to undermine the majority, and requiring workers at unionized branches to make up cash shortages from their own pockets, while not imposing this rule at non-unionized branches.

To varying degrees, employers count on the law and the police to support them in their opposition to unions. One of the most dramatic examples of this was the United Auto Workers' strike at Fleck Automotive Wire Manufacturing Company in 1978. Working conditions were deplorable for the 120 workers (mostly women, many immigrants), yet the wire shop employees did not finally consider unionizing until the company installed a spy in the women's washroom. A long and hostile certification and first-contract settlement process occurred, including a six-month strike. It was estimated that the additional cost for the police called in by the employer in its anti-union struggle was $2 million.[37]

Workplace design and structure, job fragmentation and relationships with co-workers and employers also play a role in the success of women's attempts to organize. Approximately 20% of women work in establishments with over 500 workers, compared with 35% of male workers, while 60% of employed women work with fewer than 200 fellow employees, compared with 45% of male workers. In some industries, women almost always work in small groups. For example, in the service industry, women work predominantly in establishments with fewer than 20 workers.[38] Such small work forces make unionization more difficult because organizing several small establishments involves more expense, more staff and more time from the union than organizing one larger bargaining unit.

Many places where women work are designed to permit the surveillance of employees. Employers erect room dividers to prevent employees having contact with one another. Video display terminals also isolate workers.

Problems often arise when workers in small companies know the owner personally and are encouraged to feel that they will be provided for as part of "one big happy family". Despite the fact that workers may not be well provided for, a paternalistic owner is sometimes successful in persuading employees that forming a union is akin to bringing a stranger into the family.[39]

Similarly, there are problems with traditional relationships between secretaries and their bosses. Advancement is often based on the promotion of the boss, rather than on the seniority or ability of the secretary. This privatizes the work experience and encourages secretaries to associate promotions with their bosses' advancement and not with their own abilities. This in turn creates a gap between secretaries and their co-workers in similar jobs.

Union Structure and Ideology

Sex is one of many factors in the trade union movement associated with differences in the degree of unionization. In their 1986 paper entitled "Gender Differences in Union Membership Preferences and Beliefs", Jack Fiorito and Charles Greer conclude that

> With some reservations, our results support the conclusion that gender differences in union membership ...can be attributed to factors other than gender.... Reservations are necessary because...some of the strongest gender effects arise from union-related variables. Specifically, female members are much less likely to perceive instrumentality than are male members. Also, negative views of union leadership appear to be more critical in determining voting intent for women.[40]

It is only logical that women who perceive a union to be hostile or apathetic to their concerns will be reluctant to join it. So despite substantial evidence of militancy and ability to organize, women are under-represented in trade union membership and grossly so in union leadership. Studies of women in the labour movement must question this contradiction and explore the characteristics of the organization and ideology of trade unions that have helped perpetuate women's disadvantages.[41]

In 1980, although women constituted 30.2% of trade unionists they made up only 17% of executive board members (EBMs). In government employees' unions, women made up 40.3% of the membership but only 11.5% of EBMs. In national unions women accounted for 42.7% of the membership and only 21.8% of EBMs, and in international unions, 18.5% of the membership but only 3.8% of EBMs are women. Only 160 of the 944 executive board members of all these unions were women.[42] The figures underline how poorly women are represented in trade union membership and executive positions.

It is well known that most employed women face a double work day, as they usually have primary responsibility for the home as well as their paid work. With the addition of union responsibilities, women active in a union can face a triple workload. Unions must make changes their structures and practices to address the problem of the triple workload. These changes should include clearer recognition of the unequal burden facing working women in society, providing child care facilities at union functions — or allowances for those who wish to make their own arrangements, holding at least some union local meetings at times that are convenient for working mothers, and increasing paid union leave for both local functions and education.

In addition to the prohibitive time demands of union work on women, the present model of union leadership discourages the participation of women. The image of a union official as an authority figure, an eloquent speaker, an expert negotiator, a gunslinger, is the role model union members are supposed to aspire to.[43] Because this image is not one that most women traditionally have been socialized to aspire to, many women do not consider running for union office.

Concerted opposition from the old boys also makes it difficult for women to attain leadership positions in large unions. Often, the same men who express concern for women's issues on the campaign platform are reluctant to make room for their union sisters in their exclusive clubs at the top. For example, at the 1984 CLC convention, six new for-women-only positions were created, but women were picked for those positions by the men in charge.[44]

As long as men dominate the staff and leadership positions of unions, women will find it hard to make their issues a priority, to motivate other women to become involved, and to gain positions of power within their unions. A report produced by the Women's Bureau of the CLC, entitled *Unions and Affirmative Action*, highlights the results of a survey conducted at the Fourth CLC National Equity Convention, held in 1983:

> It is interesting that not one single local without either an equality committee or women on the bargaining team, included women's issues as bargaining items. Conversely, eliminating the 8 locals where women's issues were not bargained because of government controls, only one local that had a women's committee and women on the negotiating team failed to address women's problems at the bargaining table.[45]

This demonstrates the need for women to achieve leadership positions within unions to see that women's issues remain a priority throughout the bargaining process.

UNIONS: HELP OR HINDRANCE?

Because unions have consistently ignored or downplayed issues critical to women, the question that arises is whether unions can be of benefit to women in the labour force. A number of feminist writers who have looked at labour organizations have concluded that unions have not only been of little benefit to women, but have had a negative influence.[46] Based on this conclusion, they advocate women-only unions. However, it can be argued that the past failures of unions to organize women, to secure union contracts that dealt with issues of particular interest to women, and to promote women into executive positions do not represent a failure peculiar to unions, but reflect the same economic and social forces that produced the inferior economic (and social) position of women in the first place.

In recent times, unions have benefited women substantially. Unions are now a major force in achieving recognition and acceptance of some fundamental women's demands, including maternity leave benefits, equal pay for work of equal value, and health and safety in the electronic office. There is also evidence that union officials are more sympathetic to women's issues than employers are. A study done for Employment and Immigration Canada found that trade unionists were four times as likely to identify women as a leading disadvantaged group than were the contractors and manufacturers interviewed. This suggests that trade unionists were at least aware of the problems faced by working women.[47]

In January 1982, Statistics Canada conducted a Work History Survey for 1981, which provided the first Canadian wage rate data for individuals. The study broke down the data by full-time and part-time workers, by sex, and by union membership. A detailed description of the survey appears in *The Labour Force*, October 1982. The study agrees with others (White 1980, Gunderson 1975) that the male/female wage differential is lower among unionized than among non-unionized workers.[48] White also concludes that about half the union contracts reviewed provided maternity leave benefits that exceeded those available to non-unionized workers.[49]

The CLC report, *Unions and Affirmative Action*, highlights some precedent-setting contract clauses negotiated for women:

■ 15 weeks' maternity leave with pay, equivalent to normal earnings for regular part-time workers (University of Toronto and Canadian Union of Public Employees);

■ bridging of service to allow for retention of seniority for up to six years while either parent leaves the work force to fulfil child care responsibilities (Manitoba Government Employees' Association);

114

- 17 weeks' maternity leave with pay, seniority accruing during leave (Ontario Public Service Employees Union);

- 17 weeks' unpaid leave after adoption of a child (Northern Telecom and the United Auto Workers).

As well, many unions have obtained clauses providing protection from sexual harassment.

A FUTURE PARTNERSHIP

At present, two schools of thought are in conflict within Canadian unions. One is the traditional school, which concentrates on bargaining and other efforts associated with work and its remuneration, the state of the economy, unemployment, the advent of microtechnology, and workers' concerns about job security. The other approach is social unionism. Although advocates of this approach also seek to improve wages and working conditions, social unionism recognizes that our well-being can depend on more than a good wage settlement. This point of view proposes that unions seek to change government and corporate policies for the benefit of working people.

The demands for equality for women affect the foundations of our economic, social, and political systems. They also strike close to the heart of traditional values concerning the family and male and female societal roles. To be effective in helping women to achieve equality in the workplace, trade unions will have to expand the definition of what constitutes a union issue and accept women's social and political goals as valid. Only in this way will union membership and participation become more attractive to working women.

Co-operation on social issues would benefit both women and the unions. To maintain its influence, the Canadian trade union movement needs to maintain its numbers, probably requiring organization of traditionally non-unionized private sector industries. The employees in this sector are predominantly women, most of whom could benefit significantly from the strength and protection afforded by a union organization.

NOTES

1. Linda Brisken, "Women and Unions in Canada: A Statistical Overview", in *Union Sisters: Women in the Labour Movement*, ed. L. Brisken and L. Yantz (Toronto: The Women's Educational Press, 1983).

2. Pradeep Kumar and Mary Lou Coates, *The Current Industrial Relations Scene in Canada: 1986* (Kingston: Industrial Relations Centre, 1986), p. 312.

3. Paul Phillips and Erin Phillips, *Women and Work: Inequality in the Labour Market* (Toronto: James Lorimer Publishers, 1983), p. 52.

4. Joan Sangster, "Women and Unions in Canada: A Review of Historical Research", *Resources for Feminist Research*, vol. 10, no. 2 (July 1981), p. 2.

5. *Ibid.*, p. 2.

6. *Ibid.*

7. Eleanor O'Connor, "Over the years", *Our Times*, vol. 4, no. 7 (September/October 1985).

8. Ruth Frager, "No Proper Deal: Women Workers and the Canadian Labour Movement, 1870-1940", in *Union Sisters*, ed. L. Brisken and L. Yantz.

9. *Ibid.*, p. 47.

10. Paul Phillips and Erin Phillips, *Women and Work*, p. 134.

11. L. Brisken and L. Yantz, *Union Sisters*, p. 49.

12. Eleanor O'Connor, "Over the Years", p. 56.

13. L. Brisken and L. Yantz, *Union Sisters*, p. 47.

14. Terry Copp, *The Anatomy of Power: The Condition of the Working Class in Montreal, 1897-1929*, cited in Julie White, *Women and Unions* (Ottawa: Canadian Advisory Council on the Status of Women, 1980), p. 3, note 8.

15. Alice Klein and Wayne Roberts, "Besieged Innocence: The 'Problem' and Problems of Working Women — Toronto 1896-1914", in *Women at Work: 1850-1930* (Toronto: The Women's Educational Press, 1974).

116

16. *Ibid.*, p. 220.

17. Joan Sangster, "Women and Unions in Canada", p. 15.

18. L. Brisken and L. Yantz, *Union Sisters*, p. 51.

19. Eleanor O'Connor, "Over the Years", p. 56.

20. Joan Sangster, "Women and Unions in Canada", p. 19.

21. *Ibid.*

22. L. Brisken and L. Yantz, *Union Sisters*, p. 53.

23. Andrew Gamble and Paul Walton, *Capitalism and Crises* (p. 81), cited in Pat Armstrong, *Labour Pains: Women's Work in Crisis* (Toronto: The Women's Educational Press, 1984), p. 49.

24. Pat Armstrong, *Labour Pains*, p. 54.

25. *Ibid.*, p. 52.

26. *Ibid.*, p. 53.

27. *Ibid.*

28. L. Brisken and L. Yantz, *Union Sisters*, p. 31.

29. Pat Armstrong, *Labour Pains*, p. 57.

30. Ontario Women's Directorate, *Fact Sheets*, August 1986.

31. Paul Phillips and Erin Phillips, *Women and Work*, p. 150.

32. Refer to chapter three, "Why Are Women Unionized Less Than Men?", in Julie White, *Women and Unions* (Ottawa: Canadian Advisory Council on the Status of Women, 1980), pp. 29-51.

33. L. Brisken and L. Yantz, *Union Sisters*, p. 33.

34. *Ibid.*, pp. 33-35.

35. Paul Phillips and Erin Phillips, *Women and Work*, p. 154.

36. Joan Sangster, "Women and Unions in Canada", p. 44.

37. Paul Phillips and Erin Phillips, *Women and Work*, p. 157.

38. Joan Sangster, "Women and Unions in Canada", p. 47.

39. L. Brisken and L. Yantz, *Union Sisters*, p. 202.

40. Jack Fiorito and Charles Greer, "Gender Differences in Union Membership Preferences and Beliefs", *Journal of Labour Research*, vol. 7, no. 2 (Spring 1986), p. 160.

41. Joan Sangster, "Women and Unions in Canada", p. 2.

42. L. Brisken and L. Yantz, *Union Sisters*, p. 39.

43. Canadian Union of Public Employees, *The Facts: Women's Issues*, vol. 7, no. 3 (May-June 1985), p. 75.

44. Eleanor O'Connor, "Over the Years", p. 57.

45. Hana Aach, *Unions and Affirmative Action*, prepared for the Canadian Labour Congress Women's Bureau (Ottawa: 1983).

46. Paul Phillips and Erin Phillips, *Women and Work*, p. 180.

47. *Ibid.*, p. 181.

48. Hana Aach, *Unions and Affirmative Action*, p. 3.

49. Julie White, *Women and Unions*, p. 51.

CHAPTER EIGHT

WORKERS' COMPENSATION

> When a person suffers a disabling injury at work, whether by accident or through disease, it can seem like the beginning of an avalanche. The pain and shock are the first things to deal with, and in some cases, the easiest. What follows may be a nightmare...long wrangles with the Workers' Compensation Board, perhaps a legal problem...decreased income, the stresses of unemployment, and perhaps no job to which to return.[1]

Workers' compensation is a major plank in the structure of protections in the workplace. When people are injured in the course of their jobs, they do not lose their income. Workers' compensation works as a social insurance program. It aids workers injured or made ill by their work or assists their dependants in the event of a fatality. The system seems straightforward enough — a claim is filed, accompanied by the appropriate information, it is scrutinized by the compensation board, and the worker or the surviving dependants receive benefits. Although the intent of the system is laudable, an increasing number of problems are coming to light. These problems call into question the effectiveness, and even the justice, of workers' compensation. Many of these problems are common to both female and male workers. Some affect women particularly, both as workers and as the dependants of men killed or disabled as a result of workplace accidents or disease.

In 1984, 34,968 workers' compensation claims from women in Ontario were settled, and almost 7,000 women received workers' compensation in Saskatchewan.[2] Over 30,000 compensation cases involving women were opened in 1985 in Quebec.[3] These statistics indicate that as many as 100,000 Canadian women are compensated annually for workplace injuries and illnesses and are therefore directly affected by the level, type and duration of income provided under compensation plans, as well as the medical and vocational rehabilitation assistance available. However, not all Canadian workers are covered by workers' compensation legislation, and a large proportion of those excluded are women.

This chapter looks at the workers' compensation system, how it works, and the problems faced by women attempting to obtain compensation for occupationally caused illnesses and injuries for themselves or their spouses and children. It also explores some of the pressures on the system and discusses changes being advocated by employees, trade unions, injured workers, governments and employers.

THE ORIGIN OF WORKERS' COMPENSATION

The history of workers' compensation legislation in Canada begins in Ontario where, until the early part of this century, employers took no responsibility for injured workers or their dependants. The only recourse for workers injured on the job was to sue the employer for negligence, a right that became available in 1886.[4]

In the early 1900s, rapid economic growth and mechanization were accompanied by a drastic increase in the number of injured workers (a 58% increase between 1900 and 1903 alone). As a result, there was also a dramatic increase in the number of workers suing their employers for negligence. Between 1905 and 1906, the number of court cases rose by 56.6%. The percentage of these that were successful also rose, from 48% to 75% in the first 15 years of this century.[5] The awards to workers were often quite large, presenting employers with unanticipated costs.[6] However, pursuing a case was time-consuming and costly, and few injured workers were able to go to court. Thousands of injured workers and their families were condemned to poverty and forced to depend on charity. Labour had for years been demanding improved protection for workers and compensation for work injuries and illnesses for years. However, action was not taken until employer groups, upset by increasingly costly court settlements, joined labour in their demands for workers' compensation.[7]

Finally, in 1910, the Ontario government appointed Chief Justice William Meredith to study all aspects of compensation. The resulting legislation set out the basic elements of a compensation scheme, elements that continue to characterize workers' compensation today:

- Compensation for workplace injuries and illnesses is a guaranteed right, regardless of fault.

- Benefits are based on lost earnings and last as long as the disability.

- Compensation is administered by an independent body.

- Employers pay for the entire scheme through a collective insurance system.

- Injured workers are no longer able to sue their employers for negligence.

The Ontario act came into force in 1915. Most other provinces enacted similar legislation within the next ten years. Prince Edward Island

and Newfoundland were slower, not creating compensation schemes until 1949 and 1951 respectively. The federal government passed the *Government Employees' Compensation Act* in 1918 to cover its employees but used the provincial compensation boards to adjudicate claims under the same conditions and rates determined by the relevant act in the province where the worker was employed.[8]

These plans remained largely unchanged for over fifty years, with only minor adjustments in the pensions paid to injured workers or their dependants and the assessments paid by employers. Mounting pressure from injured workers and labour organizations led to major re-evaluations of compensation schemes in some provinces in the 1970s. British Columbia, Quebec and New Brunswick made major changes in their systems, integrating occupational health and safety legislation and administration with workers' compensation.[9] However, the basic principles set out by Meredith — no-fault, employer-financed compensation — were left untouched.

WHO IS COVERED

Workers' compensation is, in theory, a compulsory scheme covering those employed in the paid labour force. However, in each province or territory, several categories of employees are excluded from coverage. These exclusions have the greatest effect on women, because they predominate in most of the occupational groups not covered.

Domestics are excluded in all but Ontario, Manitoba and the Northwest Territories. Teachers are not covered in seven provinces. Medical and para-medical personnel are not covered in eight jurisdictions, and hairdressers are excluded in four. Agricultural workers lack coverage in six provinces. Office workers are not always covered, especially if they are not attached to an industrial or manufacturing concern, leaving thousands of women who work as medical and legal secretaries, bank employees and insurance clerks without compulsory compensation coverage. In five jurisdictions, women employed in family businesses are also excluded.

For groups not covered by law, all compensation boards allow employers to apply for inclusion. Saskatchewan and Newfoundland also allow employees to request coverage. However, the boards are not compelled to grant coverage. In all cases except Quebec, the board or the provincial cabinet can regulate the inclusion of occupational groups.

Workers' compensation was established to compensate workers in the paid labour force for loss of income, so that no coverage exists for women or men outside the paid work force. Consequently, the large number of women who work as homemakers and volunteers are not included. There is no compensation for the many household hazards faced by women working in the home. Families that suffer health damage from exposure to substances such as asbestos brought home on work clothes are also not covered by workers' compensation.

HOW A CLAIM IS ESTABLISHED

Establishing a compensation claim is, on the surface, a simple procedure. The worker reports the accident or disease to the employer and/or the doctor, who fills out the proper forms and sends them to the compensation board. The board reviews the claim and starts to pay. The majority of cases of work injury are this simple and straightforward. However, not all claims proceed so smoothly, particularly those for occupational disease.

The original compensation system stated clearly that if there was a question about the cause of the accident or illness, the benefit of the doubt should be given to the worker. The burden of proof lay with the employer to prove that the workplace was not responsible for the worker's disability. However, many individuals are believed to have taken advantage of the benefits available when in fact they had no health problems or the injury had not occurred at the workplace. As a result, workers suffering from occupational diseases or musculo-skeletal problems (which may occur following long-term exposure to unhealthy working conditions and are therefore hard to diagnose as related to the workplace) face real difficulty having their claims recognized by the compensation boards. The boards are often criticized for the fact that instead of exhausting all avenues to help workers establish such claims, they adopt an adversary role, denying claims and discounting expert medical opinion that is contrary to the views of the board's doctors.

New forms of injury and disease also exist in the technologically advanced workplace; many occur in offices where large numbers of female employees are concentrated. Because these are mainly non-physical occupations, women face additional problems in having their occupational health problems recognized by boards. For example, since 1980, seven claims involving VDT-related health problems have been filed in Canada, and four of the seven have been denied. Of those denied, three involved eye injuries — cataracts and cornea damage. In each case, the worker's physician diagnosed that her work on VDTs either caused or contributed to her condition. Despite this evidence, as well as growing world-wide concern in the scientific community about the health effects of VDTs, the boards denied the claims. Benefit of the doubt was not accorded to these women. The three successful cases involved repetitive strain injuries to the hand and wrist (carpal tunnel syndrome and tenosynovitis), though one woman's claim was originally denied and later won on appeal.[10]

Retail clerks in British Columbia have faced tremendous difficulties in obtaining compensation for repetitive motion injuries. Their union handles as many as 120 appeals at any given time. Yet they have been successful in over three-quarters of the cases after waiting for a year and a half or longer at the appeal stage. Their submission to the British Columbia Federation of Labour 1985 inquiry into the workers' compensation system details the reluctance and even hostility with which the B.C. Compensation Board has approached these claims. More than 40 published reports in the medical literature and a health survey of 1,700 clerks and cashiers have been ignored by the Board. According to the union, the typical denial letter states, "There was no particular incident reported, there was no unaccustomed activity, and Board Medical Advisors do not believe the job tasks involved could cause such a condition."[11] A CBC news report about the problems retail clerks have in obtaining compensation stated that these workers, the majority of whom are women, lift more weight per year than hard rock miners — 7,000 pounds per hour, or more than one and three-quarter million pounds per year.[12]

Back injuries are another area where benefit of the doubt is often denied the worker. Approximately 50% of compensation cases involving hospital workers, who have in recent years won the nickname "white miners", relate to back disorders. Back problems that result from years of wear and tear are more problematic than those that result from a sudden accident. This is because, according to a management manual, "the cause of back injury is often difficult to determine with any degree of certainty."[13] If there is any doubt, compensation is usually denied. In British Columbia, back injuries account for 50% of all appeals.[14]

Proving the work-relatedness or causality of diseases to the satisfaction of compensation boards is a serious problem for workers. While some diseases can be readily connected with particular substances, most cannot. Many boards have schedules of recognized occupational diseases, most of which are associated with heavy industry and recognized only after long struggles by the unions on behalf of their members. If a disease is not on the schedule, the worker must prove that it was caused by the work.

For example, three women working for the federal government claimed compensation and return of their sick leave credits. These women suffered from a variety of debilitating respiratory illnesses, which their doctors diagnosed as resulting from the air in the building where they worked in Hull, Quebec. All three claims were initially denied by the Commission de la santé et de la sécurité du travail du Québec, but two of the women appealed successfully. However, because these cases would set precedents with potentially far-reaching consequences, the federal government is appealing both.[15]

The hazards of new technology — such as anaesthetic gases, VDT emissions, and indoor air pollutants — are not recognized by compensation boards, and their victims go uncompensated. Critics of compensation board policies agree that occupational disease and non-accident disability are grossly undercompensated. One Canadian expert, Terrance Ison, contends that only 20% of workplace disability is compensated.[16]

A successful claim by a Quebec worker has paved the way for recognition of another occupational health problem experienced particularly by women. She claimed that the sexual harassment at her work was an occupational injury. Her employer is appealing the decision. Inspired by this case, an Ontario worker is filing a similar claim.[17]

When a compensation claim is refused or terminated arbitrarily by a board, workers in all jurisdictions have the automatic right to appeal the board's decision. All boards have three levels of appeal, the first being an internal review of a negative decision by more senior officials. The second and third levels must be initiated by the claimant, and are usually heard by members of the compensation board. However, there is a growing trend to have third-level appeals heard by external bodies. Quebec now uses its Social Affairs Commission and Nova Scotia an Appeal Board, and Ontario is currently establishing an Appeal Tribunal. Most provinces also have medical review panels to decide purely medical appeals. Saskatchewan and British Columbia allow the worker to select one of the doctors on the review panel.

It is always in the worker's interest to appeal, since boards have been criticized for turning down claims for trivial reasons, such as incorrectly completed forms. However, so many appeals are lost that claimants have turned to provincial ombudsmen for help in changing a board's final decision. Provincial ombudsmen across Canada report workers' compensation complaints as their largest single area of concern. In 1980, the Ontario ombudsman assigned 14 full-time investigators to deal with a 400-case backlog, and new cases arrive at the rate of 40 per month.[18] In most provinces, the ombudsman cannot overturn a board's ruling and must rely on persuasion. However, in Alberta, the provincial cabinet can impose the ombudsman's decision on the board.

It must also be noted that workers or surviving spouses must investigate and pursue their entitlements on their own. The compensation boards do not seek out workers or surviving spouses to determine whether they are eligible for compensation, and in many cases, employers will not act unless prodded.

WHAT DOES COMPENSATION INCLUDE?

The basic services provided under workers' compensation legislation across Canada are the same:

- medical treatment and rehabilitation;

- vocational rehabilitation;

124

- temporary and permanent disability payments; and

- survivor's benefits to spouses and dependants.

However, the extent and level of these benefits and services vary dramatically from one jurisdiction to another.

Medical Aid and Vocational Rehabilitation

Once a claim is approved, all medical treatment required as a result of a workplace-related accident or illness is paid for by the workers' compensation board (WCB). This includes doctors' and dentists' fees, drugs, hospital fees, and prosthetic appliances. All medical aid is subject to the board's supervision and control. A worker must submit to any medical examination or test required by the board or risk losing compensation. After the claim has been approved, an injured worker may not change doctors without approval of the board, even if dissatisfied with treatment. It is easy to see why WCBs are careful in their review of claims. Once it has approved a claim, the board is required to cover what may be considerable costs.

Emphasis is placed, in policy and in practice, on returning injured workers to their jobs as quickly as possible, and many Boards have their own rehabilitation centres, including ones in Alberta, British Columbia, New Brunswick, and Ontario. Other boards purchase physical rehabilitation services from local institutions. Where it is not available locally, most boards have the discretion to send injured workers out of province for very specialized treatment. The access to physical rehabilitation services and the quality of services vary from one jurisdiction to another, and decisions about them are at the discretion of board officials.

If the illness or injury prohibits the worker from returning to her or his original job, vocational rehabilitation may be undertaken. Vocational rehabilitation is to be distinguished from medical rehabilitation and can take various forms: aptitude, skill, and intelligence testing; career counselling and résumé writing; assertiveness training; job placement; on-the-job training placement with or without subsidized wages; educational retraining (vocational or academic); and relocation. Vocational services and their extent vary drastically across Canada and are usually made available only where the injury or disease prevents a worker from returning to her former job. "Their mandate is to work with the employee to develop the most effective and least expensive plan for getting them back to work."[19]

Widows or other dependants of deceased workers may also be eligible for vocational and academic assistance, such as moving expenses, legal services to handle the sale of a home and settle the estate, schooling, counselling, and so on. However, many women are not aware that they might qualify for such assistance.

Criticism of rehabilitation services is levelled primarily at vocational services. The problem stems from the fact that workers do not have the right to rehabilitation or job security, since the services are entirely discretionary and therefore depend to a large degree on a favourable relationship between the counsellor and the claimant.[20]

The subjective nature of the vocational rehabilitation offered by the compensation boards can lend itself to discrimination against women, based on what is considered to be suitable work for women. Benefits are suspended for workers who refuse "suitable" employment or training programs suggested by the board. Women run the risk of being placed in traditional low-paying jobs, and if they refuse the board's proposal, they may lose their benefits.

Consequently, a woman may have to ensure that she obtains a rehabilitation consultant who understands the claimant's life, her aspirations, and her needs. Educational upgrading, which might involve some years of schooling and considerable money, is usually resisted by WCBs, especially if a woman is in her middle-age or older, is perceived to be an unskilled, low-wage earner, or is thought not to require the same future economic independence as a man. It is not uncommon to see long-time general duty nurses with injured backs being denied educational upgrading to allow them to move into hospital teaching or administrative work.[21]

Injured workers may find it difficult to get work because employers are reluctant to hire a worker who might be prone to re-injury, because collective agreements might prevent an injured worker from getting a suitable job for which she does not have seniority, or because no suitable employment may be available. Moreover, once the board decides a worker is fit for employment, compensation benefits cease. "The availability of employment is not really a consideration."[22] However, Quebec is an exception, because in that province, the employer of the worker suffering from injury or disease is required, under certain circumstances, to provide employment once the worker is considered ready to start work again.

Unions are demanding full rehabilitation, including retraining, with built-in job protection requiring employers to re-hire injured workers, with any loss of pay being compensated by the WCB. This would prevent situations such as the nurse who, unable to continue nursing because of a disabling back injury, was advised by the WCB to take a clerical job in a doctor's office at $6 an hour.[23]

The Ontario, British Columbia, and Alberta boards offer preventive rehabilitation services to workers who are at risk of re-injury or further exposure to a particular substance in their former jobs. This applies currently to such conditions as lung disease resulting from mineral dust exposure (asbestos and silica), vibration-induced white finger, and allergic

126

contact dermatitis (a skin condition common to women who work in kitchens and laundries and as cleaners). Assistance can be generous, including retraining, relocation, and rehabilitation allowances.

There are many women workers who could benefit from such preventive assistance, such as those who suffer from carpal tunnel syndrome and tenosynovitis (as a result of repetitive hand work such as typing or punching cash registers for extended periods) or eye strain from work with a video display terminal.

Income Replacement and Pensions

Workers' compensation was designed to provide income to workers injured or made ill by their work. There are two categories of payments: temporary benefits (which are also paid permanently to workers who are totally disabled) and permanent pensions for the partially disabled. All benefits paid under workers' compensation are tax-exempt.[24]

Temporary benefits are paid to a worker immediately following an accident or illness claim approved by the compensation board. Payments continue until the disabled worker can return to work or until he or she has attained the maximum recovery, according to the board. However, if the worker is totally disabled and cannot return to work, the pension awarded will be the same as the temporary benefit. Rates and methods of calculation of benefits differ greatly from one jurisdiction to another, as shown in the examples in Figure 8.1. As of 1985, a temporarily disabled single worker with no dependants who earned $25,000 a year in Quebec would receive compensation of $303.92 per week, while the same person with the same salary in Saskatchewan would receive $360.58 — or a difference of almost $3,000 a year.

Permanent partial disability payments are paid to workers who do not recover fully from a workplace injury or illness. The compensation board determines the extent of the permanent disability and awards a pension according to a prescribed formula. Most boards use the traditional method of determining the percentage of disability and calculate the pension by applying this percentage to the lost wages. The disabled worker then receives a monthly pension based on this calculation. This method is commonly referred to as the meat chart, since it provides so much for an eye disability, so much for a leg disability, so much for a back disability, and so on. This approach does not take into account the extent to which the disability affects the person's life or ability to work. For example, the hand of a word processor is worth more to her in terms of her work than the hand of a radio announcer, but under the present system, the same pension would be awarded.

Figure 8.1   Weekly Benefits for a Temporarily Disabled Worker
Annual Earnings of $25,000, 1985

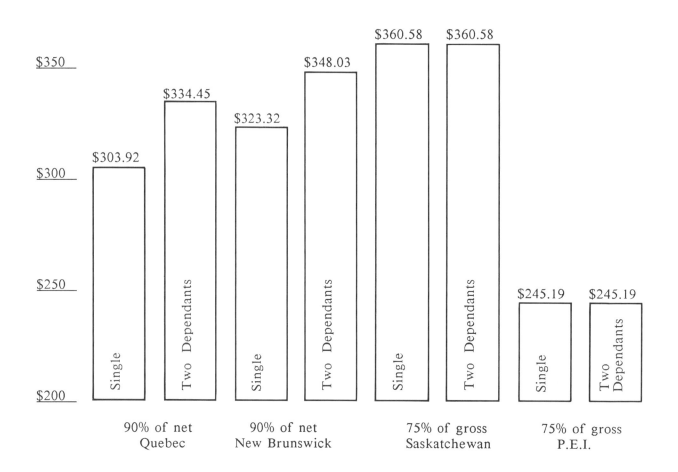

Quebec: 90% of net means both federal and provincial taxes, QPP and UIC deducted.

New Brunswick: 90% of net means federal tax, CPP and UIC deducted, but not provincial tax.

Saskatchewan: 75% of gross earnings.

Prince Edward Island: 75% of gross earnings. However, the award is based on an earnings ceiling of $17,000.

Source: Public Service Alliance of Canada, "Gross Injustices", PSAC Position Paper on Federal Workers' Compensation, June 1985.

The provinces of Saskatchewan, Newfoundland and New Brunswick have adopted a different approach to permanent partial disability compensation, based on lost wages resulting from the disability. A worker might be partially disabled, but if she can perform her pre-injury job fully, she will not receive a pension, just a one-time lump-sum payment. In these cases, however, the amounts involved are, for the most part, far smaller than under the old scheme. For example, the Public Service Alliance of Canada (PSAC) calculated that one of its members, employed in Manitoba at a salary of $25,000 and with a 17% disability, would receive $265.63 a month on the old system. Under the new wage-loss approach, the same person employed in Saskatchewan would receive a lump-sum award of between $500 and $15,000. However, the injured worker in Manitoba would receive the equivalent of the maximum Saskatchewan payment of $15,000 in just four and a half years — and her pension would continue for life.[25]

For both temporary and permanent payments, regardless of the calculation method used, two additional factors affect the amount awarded to a victim of an occupational illness or injury: whether the benefit is calculated as a percentage of gross or net wages, and the existence of ceilings on the amount of wages that can be replaced by compensation.

Traditionally, compensation was calculated at 75% of the injured worker's gross earnings (before taxes and other deductions). While some jurisdictions still use this method, there is a growing trend to calculating benefits on the basis of 90% of net earnings. Quebec, Alberta, New Brunswick and Ontario have already adopted this approach.

Though it might appear at first glance that 90% of net earnings would result in higher compensation payments, this is not always the case. It depends on which deductions are made to arrive at a net earnings amount (Figure 8.1). In a study by the Public Service Alliance of Canada, it is estimated that "a worker without dependants in Quebec [which uses the 90% of net calculation method] would receive approximately $3,000 [per year] less than in Saskatchewan [which uses 75% of gross] based on identical earnings" because, after all the deductions, the net amount is so much lower than the gross.[26]

The second factor affecting benefits is the ceiling imposed by each province, representing the maximum earnings on which compensation will be based. These range from a low of $17,000 a year in Prince Edward Island to a maximum of $45,000 in Newfoundland. Most are in the $20,000 to $30,000 range and are adjusted from time to time. Thus, a worker's compensation benefits may bear no relation to her actual earnings, resulting in severe economic penalty, particularly in the provinces with very low ceilings. The maximum weekly benefits in Newfoundland are almost $350 a week higher than in Prince Edward Island.[27]

The compensation schemes generally base both temporary wage-loss rates and permanent pensions on a worker's actual earnings (up to the ceiling) at the date of injury or first disablement from disease. Alternatively, the income replacement level can be set at a rate other than the actual wage rate at the date of injury, by taking into account the worker's income for two, three, or more years before the date of disablement.

However, in some provinces, the statutes allow for the worker's future potential earning capacity to be taken into account. This is of particular importance where a worker is injured seriously at her first low-paying job or early in her working life and a pension for permanent disability is at issue. Women who are just returning to work after childrearing, who have low-paying or entry-level jobs, or who work part-time are seriously disadvantaged by a compensation system that measures their present and future income loss only by their actual wages at the date of injury.

When a worker dies of an injury or disease that is work-related, the surviving spouse and/or other dependants are entitled to a pension. The pensions awarded, and the methods of calculation, are not consistent across the country. An increasing number of provincial boards award pensions to dependent surviving spouses on the basis of the pension the deceased worker would have received if totally disabled. Alberta and Manitoba give the full amount; British Columbia, New Brunswick and Quebec determine the percentage according to the number of dependent children. A few jurisdictions still award a fixed monthly pension to the widow(er) with an additional amount for each child under 16 or 18 years of age. These amounts bear no relation to the deceased spouse's earnings and are notoriously low. Pensions are usually awarded for life or until the person remarries. In addition to monthly pensions, most provinces award a lump-sum payment and have provisions for funeral allowances. These amounts range from approximately $40,000 in Newfoundland and Ontario to less than $1,000 in New Brunswick and Prince Edward Island. Most are less than $3,000.[28]

In recent years, a number of provinces have taken steps to end what is called the stacking of benefits, which occurs when survivor benefits are received from the Canada or Quebec Pension Plan or other sources in addition to the benefits from workers' compensation. The trend to eliminate stacking adds to financial hardship, because any C/QPP or other pension benefits are deducted from the amount paid under workers' compensation. This is certainly a backward step for women and other low-wage earners, whose pensions are already below poverty levels. Also, a change to the *Income Tax Act* has made workers' compensation pensions reportable as income under the Guaranteed Income Supplement program. This has resulted in reduced incomes for many Canadians over 65 years of age.

130

Economic frustration resulting from low benefit levels and moral indignation at being financially penalized are leading to increasing criticism of workers' compensation by injured workers and organized labour. Injured workers' groups have sprung up across the country in the last decade to pressure WCBs to improve benefit levels. The practice of some boards of tying pensions to the percentage of disability, rather than to the actual lost earnings as a result of the disability, has meant poverty for many workers. Even the provinces that compensate according to the wage-loss system do not pay workers the full amount of their former earnings.

Only four provinces index pensions; most of the others have only periodic increases, and these have not kept pace with inflation. Moreover, only three boards regularly upgrade the wage rate on which the claimant's pension is calculated, to reflect rising wages in the person's occupation. In effect, workers are being penalized financially for being injured or made ill by their work.

Organization, research and vigorous advocacy are needed to promote workers' compensation for widows and widowers. There are no national, provincial or regional organizations for these people, whose lives are affected profoundly by what happens to their spouses at work and how they are dealt with by compensation boards after workplace accidents and illnesses. Many should be eligible for compensation benefits, but the Ontario Federation of Labour estimates that more than $650 million is not paid to families of cancer victims alone.[29]

ALTERNATIVE BENEFITS AND OPTIONS

A worker suffering from a work-related health impairment may be eligible for benefits other than workers' compensation. In most cases, these must be repaid if a WCB claim is accepted.

If unionized, a worker may qualify for sick-leave and long-term disability benefits under her/his collective agreement. Where a workers' compensation claim has not yet been accepted, or if its termination is being appealed, many collective agreements cover the disabled worker until it is resolved. Sometimes, the collective agreement benefits are better than the workers' compensation benefits. However, the employer or the insurance carrier might refuse to pay if the worker is also eligible (though not receiving) for compensation from the WCB. In such cases, the worker can file a grievance through her/his union.

Unemployment Insurance benefits are available to a person who is off work because of a work-related disability. However, these benefits are paid for a maximum of 15 weeks.

Canada/Quebec Pension Plan (C/QPP) disability benefits may

provide income for a person suffering from "a severe and prolonged mental or physical disability" that prevents her from working. However, she must have contributed to the C/QPP for a total of seven years, including five of the last ten, to be eligible for benefits. It is more difficult for women to meet these eligibility requirements if they have been out of the paid labour force for a period of childrearing. In 1985, the maximum payment for a single adult was approximately $414 per month, plus $90 per month for each dependant — generally far lower than WCB pensions for total disability. In most provinces, the C/QPP survivor's pension is now deducted from the WCB survivor's pension.

Provincial welfare schemes also have disability allowances. These will not usually pay out benefits where workers' compensation is being paid, unless the WCB pension is very low. The amounts paid vary from province to province, but all are well below the poverty level.

Workers who are seriously disabled by disease or accident at work may be able to sue an employer for using defective equipment or toxic substances. However, such suits have seldom been pursued, since court action is expensive and time-consuming, and damage awards have not been generous enough to warrant the time and expense of a court case.

INCREASED COSTS AND UNFUNDED LIABILITY

Employers and governments are becoming increasingly concerned about the financial problems facing the compensation system. The 12 provincial and territorial schemes are facing a $5 billion unfunded liability (the difference between the amount collected from employers in premiums and the cost of meeting future compensation claims). This is because boards have failed to set employers' assessment rates high enough. In fact, for two years in the 1970s, the Ontario board reduced rates, yet claim costs continued to rise, and the Board failed to allow for future inflation.[30] In the face of this financial crunch, many employers are protesting loudly. They are unwilling to pay the large increases that would be necessary to reduce the unfunded liability. "Most want it to be somebody else's problem"[31] and are looking to the government to bail them out.

Some blame "do-gooder boards that are handing out their money with liberal abandon."[32] Others are calling for the boards to cut expenses. The President of the Employers' Council of British Columbia "told the Workers' Compensation Board in July to cut costs by denying compensation for occupational diseases because it's hard to tell what causes diseases and there are hazardous substances everywhere, not just in the workplace."[33]

The trend away from the old pension-for-life approach and toward the wage-loss system is attributable in part to this pressure to reduce costs. However, experts agree that costs are likely to rise steeply as

132

occupational disease claims increase. One estimate is that Ontario's bill could rise by $150 million per year.[34]

Governments have not indicated a readiness to step in and make major changes. However, it must be remembered that the present WCB system was not established until employers could no longer tolerate compensation costs and began to exert pressure on legislators. Some employers are now beginning to advocate a universal sickness-and-accident plan to shift some of the financial burden to the taxpayer. Sooner or later, governments will be forced to make a choice — cut compensation benefits and services, force employers to pay the full cost, or develop a new system.

CONCLUSION

The compensation system in Canada is fraught with problems, and pressure is mounting from both workers and employers for drastic change. Workers' major complaints fall into four categories: inadequate benefits, benefit of the doubt being denied to workers, lack of adequate recognition of occupational disease, and inadequate and arbitrarily available rehabilitation services.

From a public policy perspective, all workers, full- or part-time, female or male, paid or unpaid, should be insured under an equitable system offering the best possible income maintenance and rehabilitation services. There is ample evidence that our compensation system does not meet these objectives for the population in general, and for women in particular.

More than half of all women are employed in the paid labour market, and their numbers continue to grow. Many of the jobs women do are hazardous. They are exposed to a wide variety of chemicals, work in uncomfortable and unhealthy conditions, endure stress, and work in buildings polluted with toxic substances. Many groups of women in the paid labour force are excluded from compensation coverage by law, and women who do not earn wages, homemakers and volunteer workers, are not even considered. Occupational diseases are not given adequate recognition by compensation boards, which often treat workers as adversaries trying to obtain benefits to which they are not entitled. Injured workers are penalized financially, do not receive adequate rehabilitation, and face numerous obstacles in finding decent jobs to return to. Many widows and widowers do not receive benefits because they do not realize that they are eligible to apply for them.

The compensation system is plagued with serious financial problems because employers' contributions were insufficient to pay for future claims, and they are justifiably unwilling to make up the difference, since it runs into billions of dollars.

In addition, occupational accident and disease statistics indicate that the compensation system does not result in increased efforts to eliminate workplace hazards. Serious charges have been made that the system allows employers to pool their risks and protects them from criminal and civil prosecution in cases of negligence.

Many critics of the system claim that the problems are too large to be solved by tinkering with existing legislation and board structures. They argue in favour of a completely new approach that would provide compensation without regard to the cause of the disability, commonly referred to as a universal sickness and accident scheme.

Universal sickness and accident plans are government-run no-fault insurance programs that would replace workers' compensation and most other disability payment schemes, including those for automobile accidents. Many models have been developed, but most provide for costs to be borne jointly by governments, employers and people paying automobile insurance premiums, according to an estimate of the proportion of disability related to the various sectors. Claims would be paid directly on proof of disability, regardless of the cause of the injury or illness or where it happened. Consequently, women working in the home or as volunteers and all women in the labour force would be covered by such a universal system. Since causality need not be proved, the current problems associated with trying to prove, for example, that back injuries were caused at work or that chemical substances at work were responsible for a disability would all be eliminated. The first such system was developed in New Zealand to cover accidents only.

The labour movement has not been enthusiastic about this proposal because of the belief that employers should pay for workplace accidents and diseases. However, proponents of the universal system argue that employers do not pay the full cost of occupationally induced disability under the current system and that there are better ways to force employers to eliminate hazards from the workplace, such as tougher safety legislation, enforcement and penalties. It can also be argued that the employer is not the only one to benefit from the labour of employees, that hazards are not always known, and that the burden of the costs of the system should be shared by all members of society.

The lessons of the past foretell major changes in the system. Some boards have already cut services to reduce costs. It is in the interests of women to consider the role that workers' compensation plays in their lives and to join with unions and other dissatisfied groups to ensure that changes meet their needs and overcome present problems.

NOTES

1. Michael Izumi Nash, *Canadian Occupational Health and Safety Handbook* (Don Mills: CCH Canadian, 1983), p. 167.

2. Robert Holden, Supervisor, Statistical Analysis Section, Workers' Compensation Board of Ontario; Ken Dusselier, Research and Information Officer, Workers' Compensation Board of Saskatchewan.

3. Carole Chamberland, head of the Division traitement et information statistique, Service de la statistique et de l'évaluation des programmes, Commission de la santé et de la sécurité du travail du Québec.

4. Theresa Jennissen, "The Development of the Workmen's Compensation Act of Ontario, 1914", *Canadian Journal of Social Work Education*, vol. 7, no. 1 (1981), p. 58.

5. *Ibid.*, p. 57, 59.

6. Michael Izumi Nash, *Canadian Occupational Health and Safety Handbook*, p. 168.

7. Theresa Jennissen, "Development of the Workmen's Compensation Act", pp. 60, 62.

8. Jim Ellsworth, "Workers' Compensation — The Federal System", in *Participate for Change*, Proceedings from the Public Service Alliance of Canada's First Health and Safety Conference (Ottawa: 1983), pp. 164-165.

9. Corpus Information Services, *Occupational Health and Safety Management Handbook* (Don Mills: 1985), p. 1.

10. Bob DeMatteo, *Terminal Shock* (Toronto: NC Press, 1985), pp. 180-182.

11. Retail Clerks Union, Local 1518 (UFAW), *Submission to the B.C. Federation of Labour Public Inquiry into the Workers' Compensation System* (Vancouver: 1985), p. 10, 13.

12. Paul Griffin, CBC Radio News, *The World at Six*, November 21, 1985.

13. Corpus Information Service, *Occupational Health and Safety*, p. 124.

14. Ken Hansen, "Workers' Compensation Crisis", *B.C. Workers' Health Newsletter*, no. 11 (September 1985), p. 7.

15. "Les Terrasses Appeal Angers Some", *The Citizen* [Ottawa], July 30, 1983.

16. Cathy Walker, quoting from Osgoode Hall Law Professor Terrance Ison's speech to the Canadian Association of Industrial Mechanical and Allied Workers' National Convention, April 27, 1985, in "Universal Disability", *B.C. Workers' Health Newsletter*, no. 11 (September 1985), p. 18.

17. Dorothy Lipovenko, "Sexual Harassment Ruled Work Injury", *The Globe and Mail* [Toronto], April 11, 1985.

18. John Deverell, "Labour Employers Want Changes — Opposite Ones", *Toronto Star*, August 16, 1980.

19. Michael Izumi Nash, *Canadian Occupational Health and Safety Handbook*, p. 179.

20. Charles Reasons, Lois Ross and Craig Paterson, *Assault on the Worker* (Toronto: Butterworths, 1981), p. 188.

21. Bernadette Stringer, *A Submission to the B.C. Federation of Labour Inquiry into the Workers' Compensation Board* (Vancouver: B.C. Nurses Union Provincial Health and Safety Committee, April 11, 1985), p. 3.

22. Timothy Taylor and Ian Mahon, *An Advocate's Guide to Workers' Compensation in Manitoba* (Winnipeg: Public Legal Education Activities/Activités d'éducation juridique populaire, Faculty of Law, University of Manitoba, 1985), pp. 24-25.

23. Bernadette Stringer, *A Submission to the B.C. Federation of Labour Inquiry*, p. 3.

24. For a detailed discussion of compensation payments, see Michael Izumi Nash, *Canadian Occupational Health and Safety Handbook*, pp. 182-189.

25. Public Service Alliance of Canada, *Gross Injustices, PSAC Position Paper on Federal Workers' Compensation* (Ottawa: 1985), p. 16.

26. *Ibid.*, p. 17.

27. *Ibid.*, p. 18.

28. Michel Gauvin, *Workers' Compensation Legislation in Canada*, 1982 Edition, Labour Canada (Ottawa: Supply and Services Canada, 1982), pp. 6-10, 30-31.

29. Ontario Federation of Labour, *Response to the Second Weiler Report, Protecting the Worker from Disability, Challenges for the Eighties* (Toronto: 1983).

30. Margaret Wente, "The Coming Crisis in Workers' Compensation", *Canadian Business* (February 1984), p. 47.

31. *Ibid.*, p. 48.

32. *Ibid.*, p. 47.

33. Cassandra Kobayashi, "More Attacks on Compensation System", *B.C. Workers' Health Newsletter*, no. 10 (December 1984), p. 1.

34. Margaret Wente, "The Coming Crisis in Workers' Compensation", p. 49.

CHAPTER NINE

THE PENSION SYSTEM

Women have a particular stake in the pension reforms that are now under way. Not only do women account for a majority of the elderly (in 1985, they were 54% of the 65 to 69 age group, and 58% of those aged 70 or older[1]), but their chances of being poor in old age are greater than those of men, particularly if they are on their own. The average income of elderly women who were single, divorced, or widowed in 1984 was only $10,080 — just 10% above the poverty line for an individual living in a large city. The average income of elderly men who were single, divorced or widowed was $13,800.[2] However, there were more than three times as many elderly women on their own as there were elderly men — a reflection of the fact that women tend to marry men older than themselves and, because women also have longer life expectancies, tend to outlive their husbands.

It is encouraging to note that the incomes of the elderly have improved in relation to other groups in the population over the past five or six years. That considerable progress has been made in the battle against poverty is thanks to government-sponsored income security programs such as Old Age Security (OAS) and the Guaranteed Income Supplement (GIS), which are described in more detail in the next section of this chapter. Between 1979 and 1984, for example, incomes of unattached elderly individuals increased by 73%, while incomes of elderly married couples rose by 76%. In comparison, the incomes of all types of families rose by only 46% during that period.[3]

The incidence of poverty among the elderly has dropped significantly. In 1984, only 11% of elderly married couples were poor, compared with 22% in 1979; and just under 50% of the single elderly were poor in 1984, compared with more than 66% in 1979.[4] Encouraging as these trends are, however, there are still large numbers of elderly women with incomes below the poverty level. Almost 59% of unattached elderly women had incomes below $9,000 in 1984.[5] In effect, then, a majority of elderly women on their own still have incomes below the poverty level.

The fact that so many of the elderly are still poor, despite extensive public and private income security programs, has been a major preoccupation in proposals for pension reform. There has been particular concern that reforms should address the retirement income needs of women, who account for the majority of the elderly and for a disproportionate number of those with low incomes. The inadequacies of the existing system are especially worrying because the elderly will form an increasing percentage of the population over the next few decades.

Most of the women who are now senior citizens spent most of their lives as full-time homemakers. Forty years ago, only 20% of all women participated in the labour force, and less than 5% of married women worked outside the home.[6] Women who are now aged 65 or older thus had little opportunity to contribute to a pension plan or to build up income for their retirement years. Many of them must rely on government programs such as OAS/GIS for their income needs, supplemented by their husbands' private pension provisions (if any) and by survivor benefits from the Canada/Quebec Pension Plan (C/QPP), which was introduced only in 1966.

However, there have been remarkable changes in the economic role of women since today's senior citizens were young. Among women between the ages of 20 and 44, more than 71% now participate in the labour force. The labour force participation rate of married women in this age group is now 68%.[7] Statistics indicate that these women will have a permanent and long-term commitment to paid employment, with only very brief interruptions for childbearing or childrearing. In all probability, these women will have the opportunity to contribute to pension plans, predominantly public plans, and to accumulate retirement savings in their own right.

Somewhere in between are the women now in their late forties and fifties. These were the mothers of the baby boom generation. The typical woman in this age group had four children, left the labour force for an extended period of time while her children were young, and may have returned to paid employment, often on a part-time basis, when her youngest child entered school. About half (48%) of all women in the 45 to 64 age group participate in the labour force, and less than 46% of married women in this age group are labour force participants.[8]

Pension reform must address the needs of women in each of these groups. To focus only on homemakers, for example, while ignoring the problems of women in paid employment, could mean that the majority of women will still end up poor in old age, for women in paid employment have inadequate pension protection under the current retirement income system. The work patterns of women have undergone a remarkable transformation in the past few decades, but the economic role of women is still in transition, and that too must be recognized in the design of a retirement income system that will meet the needs of women in a variety of situations.

WOMEN AND THE CURRENT RETIREMENT INCOME SYSTEM

The existing retirement income system has three main components, with different objectives, different implications for women, and different effects on them. The main components are often described as *tiers* and can be thought of as building blocks that individuals use to plan their retirement incomes.

The First Tier — A Basic Guarantee

The first building block or tier is designed to provide a basic minimum guaranteed annual income for all elderly people. Three federal programs and various provincial supplements combine to meet this anti-poverty objective, although they may fall somewhat short of meeting it in some circumstances.

Old Age Security (OAS), often referred to as the old age pension, is a flat-rate benefit that goes to all those who reach the age of 65, provided they meet certain residency requirements. To get the full OAS benefit, worth about $300 a month, a person must have lived in Canada for at least 40 years after her/his eighteenth birthday. Those who cannot meet this requirement get a reduced benefit — a measure that can be particularly hard on immigrants who have no other form of retirement income. OAS benefits are indexed to the Consumer Price Index, are adjusted every quarter, and are taxable.

The Guaranteed Income Supplement (GIS) is another federal benefit paid to those who qualify on the basis of an income test. Assets are not taken into account in determining eligibility. Therefore, an elderly person might own a home but still qualify for GIS if he or she has little or no income other than OAS. Benefits are also indexed, and different rates are paid according to marital status. The amount of the monthly benefit depends on the pensioner's other income. The maximum GIS benefit in July 1986 was $346 for a single person; the maximum for a married couple was $226 a month for each spouse. GIS benefits are not taxable.

Taken together, the maximum annual benefit a single individual could obtain from OAS/GIS in July 1986 was $7,650. For a married couple, the maximum annual benefit from these two programs was $12,411. It is estimated that the poverty level for a single individual living in a city of more than 500,000 population in 1986 was about $10,600, while the poverty level for a couple was about $14,000.[9] The basic guaranteed income from OAS/GIS thus comes much closer to meeting the anti-poverty objective for couples than it does for single people. These inadequacies have particularly serious implications for women, since they account for more than three-quarters of all unattached elderly persons, and they are much less likely than men are to have other sources of income.[10]

British Columbia, Alberta, Manitoba, Saskatchewan, Ontario, Nova Scotia and both territories also have income supplements for the aged, but the amounts vary considerably from one jurisdiction to another. In some provinces, each spouse gets a higher benefit than an individual alone, thus widening the disparity between singles and couples already evident in OAS/GIS. In 1984, the maximum annual supplement for a single individual ranged from a low of $219 in Nova Scotia to a high of $1,200 in the Yukon. No supplements are paid at all in Newfoundland, New Brunswick, Prince Edward Island and Quebec.[11]

There is one other federal program that forms part of the first tier of retirement income. Called the Spouse's Allowance, it was originally designed to provide a benefit to spouses who had not yet reached the age of 65 but were married to pensioners who qualified for GIS. The intention was that a low-income couple where one spouse was between the ages of 60 and 65 would be able to receive benefits equivalent to the OAS/GIS benefits to which a couple is entitled if both spouses are over 65.

However, the Spouse's Allowance was recently made available to all low-income individuals between the ages of 60 and 65, provided they meet the income test, but only if they are widows or widowers. Individuals who qualify but are single or divorced are not eligible for benefits. The program has been heavily criticized because it discriminates on the grounds of marital status. It is likely that legal challenges will eventually be made.

It must be emphasized that the first tier of the retirement income system is intended to provide a guaranteed annual income to all senior citizens, regardless of whether they had paid employment prior to age 65. For women who spent their lives as full-time homemakers, this part of the pension system gives them a pension in their own name once they reach age 65, although as we have seen, the amount of the basic guarantee is inadequate, especially for those who do not have a spouse.

The Second Tier — Income Replacement

The objective of the second tier of the retirement income system is to provide a replacement income when people retire from paid employment, so that their income in retirement does not fall too far below their pre-retirement income. This allows them to avoid a precipitous drop in their standard of living once they retire. This income replacement objective is met partly by government-sponsored pension plans (sometimes called public pensions) in the second tier and partly by private arrangements, which form the third tier and are described in the next section.

By definition, pensions in the second tier of the system are related to earnings, since their purpose is to replace some percentage of those earnings when a worker retires and thus ceases to work for pay. The

142

government-sponsored plans are the Canada Pension Plan, which operates everywhere except in Quebec, and the Quebec Pension Plan, which is virtually the same as the Canada Pension Plan and is administered by the province of Quebec for residents of that province.

By law, everyone who is in the paid labour force, whether as an employee or self-employed, must contribute a percentage of their earnings to either the Canada Pension Plan (CPP) or the Quebec Pension Plan (QPP). While the first $2,000 or so of earnings — the amount known as the Yearly Basic Exemption (YBE) — is exempt from contributions, employees must contribute 1.9% of their earnings above that, up to maximum earnings of about $26,000. This amount, known as the Yearly Maximum Pensionable Earnings or YMPE, and the YBE are indexed to rise each year. The YMPE is roughly equivalent to the average wage earned by industrial workers. CPP and QPP contributions by employees are matched by an equal amount from the employer. Self-employed persons must contribute 3.8% of earnings within the same limits.

These contribution rates have been in effect since the C/QPP started in 1966. In 1987, however, rates started to increase gradually to reach a level of 7.6% (3.8% for employees and 3.8% for employers) by the year 2011. The changes are among several reforms to the C/QPP introduced in 1986. Higher contribution rates are needed because, as the elderly form an increasing percentage of the population over the next 20 to 30 years, more money will be needed to pay for their pensions. At present, the CPP fund has more than enough money to pay the pensions of people who are retiring. The surplus funds have been invested in provincial government bonds — in effect the money has been lent to the provinces. If provinces were to repay the money they have borrowed, there would be no need to increase contributions until the beginning of the next century. However, federal and provincial governments have apparently decided that provinces should not have to repay the money borrowed and that increased contribution rates should be phased in over a period of time.

The amount of benefits people receive from the C/QPP depends on their earnings and contribution record. Basically, one may expect to receive 25% of average annual earnings, subject to the limits outlined earlier. Earnings are averaged over the individual's working life from age 18 to age 65. To allow for periods of unemployment or interruptions in paid employment resulting from further training or education, contributors may exclude 15% of their working years in calculating the average earnings on which the pension will be based. In addition, parents may exclude periods when they cared for a child under the age of seven. This provision was designed to assist women who leave the labour force temporarily to look after a child, although it is important to note that one does not have to leave the labour force in order to claim this benefit. It may be claimed for any years when children are under the age of seven. Therefore, those who worked part-time or had low earnings when their children were young can

143

also leave those years out of the calculation. Technically, the provision is available to either parent, but it goes to the person who received the Family Allowance on behalf of the child; in other words, it is usually the mother who benefits.

The maximum retirement benefit available under the C/QPP is now $527 a month, but most women who retire from paid employment receive much less than this because their earnings are generally below the average. It should be noted that even people who are entitled to the maximum C/QPP retirement benefit may still qualify for some GIS benefits if they have no other income apart from C/QPP and OAS.

In addition to retirement benefits, the C/QPP also provides disability pensions and benefits for children of disabled contributors, as well as for dependent children of deceased contributors. Of particular interest to women are the benefits for surviving spouses, which are discussed later in this chapter. Women who have been full-time homemakers may thus be entitled to a pension from the C/QPP, either as the surviving spouse of a contributor or as the divorced spouse of a contributor (a provision that is also explained later).

The Third Tier — Private Pension Arrangements

The third building block in the retirement income system consists of private arrangements that people make for retirement, either through their employers or on their own. Many employers establish pension plans for their employees; often these arrangements are negotiated through the collective bargaining process. Private pension arrangements are also related to earnings, and the objective is to ensure the maintenance of a certain standard of living when a worker retires from paid employment.

The major problem with this part of the retirement income system as far as women are concerned is that the majority of women do not have access to employer-sponsored pension plans. In 1984, for example, only 37% of women who were in paid employment, and 54% of men who were working for pay, were members of an employer-sponsored (or private) pension plans.[12] The main reason for such low coverage of women in paid employment is that most work in sectors of the economy, such as trade and personal service, where employers do not usually have employee benefit programs. Many employers in these sectors are small businesses, which claim it would be too expensive for them to provide pensions and other benefits. Also, about 26% of women in paid employment work part-time (only 8% of men are part-time workers).[13] Part-time workers are usually excluded from pension plans, even when one is provided for full-time employees.

Of course, women who are not in the work force are not covered by employer-sponsored pension plans, except insofar as they may receive

144

benefits as the surviving spouse of a deceased contributor or as the divorced spouse of a contributor. However, 43% of private pension plans do not provide a benefit for a surviving spouse. Even in those plans where this option is available, many contributors decide against it because it would mean accepting a lower initial retirement benefit.

There are two main types of employer-sponsored pension plans. The defined benefit plan is one in which the worker is promised a specific benefit, usually expressed as a percentage of salary for each year of service. In the federal public service, for example, an employee receives 2% of average annual earnings over the six best earning years for each year of service. An employee who worked for the federal government for 30 years would thus receive a retirement benefit equivalent to 60% of her or his average annual earnings over the six years of highest earnings. About 95% of all pension plan members belong to defined benefit plans. Actuaries calculate what percentage of earnings must be contributed to the plan by employers and employees in order to pay the benefits promised, taking into account the amount those contributions are likely to earn over the period before pensions have to be paid. Regardless of how these calculations turn out to be, a defined benefit plan undertakes to pay the promised benefit when the employee retires.

The defined contribution plan is one where contributions are specified as a percentage of earnings, but no particular level of benefits is promised. Employee and employer contributions are invested in a fund, and whatever the fund has earned by the time the employee reaches retirement age is used to buy a pension for the employee. For this reason, these plans are sometimes referred to as money purchase plans. Because the employer does not undertake to provide a particular level of benefits, their cost to the employer is predictable and often quite low. As a result, money purchase plans are popular with smaller employers; they are easier to administer and less costly. For employees, however, the lack of a set level of benefits offers little security for retirement. While there are many small money purchase plans, only about 5% of all pension plan members belong to this type of plan.

Both defined benefit and money purchase plans present particular problems for women. In a defined benefit plan, employees usually do not establish a right to the benefit promised by the employer (called vesting) until they have worked for the employer at least 10 years. They may also have to have reached the age of 45. Since women tend to change jobs more frequently than men do, their pensions are less likely to be vested when they leave a particular employer, in which case they get back only what they have contributed to the plan, often with little or no interest. Moreover, few pension plans are portable — enabling an employee to transfer pension credits built up in the former employer's plan to the new employer's plan.

Where benefits are vested before the employee leaves a job, she will receive a pension at retirement from that employer. However, because benefits are not likely to be adjusted for inflation, the pension may not be worth very much by the time the employee receives it. Lack of inflation adjustment can be especially serious for women because their greater longevity means they will probably have to exist for a longer period on an inadequate pension.

Money purchase plans are also disadvantageous for women because of the way benefits are calculated. Funds in the plan at the time of retirement are used to buy a pension annuity (usually in the form of a monthly benefit) for the retiring employee. However, where a woman and a man have the same amount in their retirement income fund, the woman will get a lower monthly benefit. The insurance companies that sell the annuities argue that because a woman is likely to live longer than a man, the companies will have to go on paying benefits for a longer period; thus the monthly pension for a woman must be smaller, it is argued, although the total pay-out is likely to be the same in both cases.

These problems in the design of private pension plans are being addressed through pension reform; the federal government and the provinces are amending their legislation governing private pension plans in their jurisdictions. In most cases, the following changes are being considered:

- vesting to occur after two years instead of the usual ten;

- governments generally will not compel employers to provide inflation protection (although some do this already); however, a number of jurisdictions will make it possible for employees to transfer their pension entitlement to a new employer or to some kind of special retirement savings account if they leave a job;

- part-time workers will generally have to be allowed to join pension plans, where these are provided for full-time employees;

- benefits for surviving spouses will be mandatory, unless both spouses agree in writing to waive this provision; and

- for money purchase plans, employers will generally be required to provide equal monthly benefits for employees who have made equal contributions.

Important as these changes are, they will still benefit only a minority of women in the work force, because such a small percentage of women in paid employment are members of private pension plans. While some have argued that improved portability (the ability to transfer benefits from one plan to another) and other measures, such as including part-time workers in pension plans, will improve the coverage of women workers by

146

private pension plans, it seems unlikely that these provisions will have a major effect. For instance, about 80% of all women who have part-time employment work in the trade and personal service sectors. Since few employers in these sectors provide pension plans for their full-time employees, part-time workers in these sectors will still not have access to pension coverage. Most women approaching retirement in the future will probably still have to rely on public pension plans (the first two tiers of the retirement income system) for most of their pension needs, unless their earnings are high enough that they can their own arrangements.

In addition to employer-sponsored pension plans, the third tier of the retirement income system includes private arrangements for retirement income made by individuals with government support. Notable among these are registered retirement savings plans (RRSPs). Individuals may contribute to these plans up to certain limits and claim a tax deduction for the entire amount of their contribution. (Employee contributions to employer-sponsored pension plans are also tax-deductible within limits.) Making contributions to RRSPs tax-deductible costs the federal government $5 billion a year in lost tax revenues, almost twice what the government spends on GIS benefits to needy pensioners.[14] However, the amount spent on tax breaks to those who make private pension arrangements goes mainly to higher-income earners. A study conducted by the Department of Finance in 1979 indicated that only one in ten people who filed tax returns and had incomes below $50,000 contributed to RRSPs, while more than 60% with incomes above $50,000 a year put money into an RRSP.[15] One reason is that because government assistance is given in the form of a tax deduction, the higher the contributor's income, the bigger the tax break. In spite of this, proposals have been presented in recent federal budgets to increase the limit on RRSP contributions. In fact, the limits will now be so high that only those whose annual incomes exceed $86,000 will be able to take full advantage of them.[16]

Although RRSP rules allow a spouse to make contributions on behalf of the other spouse, very few women contribute to RRSPs on their own behalf, and when they do, their lower incomes mean they cannot afford to contribute as much as men do. Only 8.5% of women who filed tax returns in 1981 contributed to an RRSP, and their average contribution was $1,630. In comparison, 16.8% of males filing tax returns contributed an average of $2,038 to their RRSPs in the same year.[17]

In summary, on average, women who are now of retirement age still get most of their retirement income from the public pension plans in the first two tiers of the retirement income system. At the same time, the data reflect the gradual improvement in the financial situation of elderly women over the past decade. In 1978, 21% of elderly women were so poor that they qualified for the full GIS benefit. By 1982, this figure had declined to 15%. However, 39% of women still received some GIS benefits — an indication that more improvements need to be made.[18]

Unattached women aged 65 or older in 1982 received 42% of their income from OAS/GIS; another 8% came from C/QPP benefits; 4% came from other government transfers; 12% came from pensions, annuities, and other income; 29% came from investment income; and 5% came from wages, salaries, and net income from self-employment.[19]

WOMEN AND PENSION REFORM ~~SOLUTIONS~~

After many years of discussions, pension reform is now under way. Changes to the Canada Pension Plan have been passed by Parliament and the provinces and came into force on January 1, 1987. The federal government and many of the provinces are also making changes in the laws governing private pension plans in their jurisdictions. However, the changes will by no means meet all the concerns of women.

In this section, we examine those concerns and the key issues that must be addressed in reform of both public and private pensions.

Better Pensions for Those Now Retired

Changes in the design of pension plans, whether public or private, will do little to help women who are already past retirement age. Many of them, as we have seen, have to rely on OAS/GIS as their main source of income. The basic minimum income guaranteed by these plans is inadequate, especially for women on their own. An increase in the total benefit, whether through an increase in OAS, an increase in GIS, or a combination of both, is needed so that those who have no other source of income in retirement are guaranteed an amount that is at least equivalent to the poverty level. At this time, for unattached individuals, it is not.

Such an improvement would benefit not only women who are now past the age of 65, but also women who spend most of their lives as full-time homemakers in the future and are therefore not able to contribute to a pension plan.

Better Pensions for Women in the Paid Work Force

The majority of women approaching retirement in the future will not be full-time homemakers. They will be women who have spent most or all of their adult lives in paid employment. Sixty-three per cent of women now in paid employment do not have access to employer-sponsored pensions. Pension reforms now being implemented are unlikely to do much to improve this low level of coverage for women workers. Thus, most women retiring in the future will probably still have to rely on the first two tiers of the

148

system for their retirement income needs. But the C/QPP pays a benefit of only 25% of average annual earnings. At present, the OAS benefit is equivalent to only 14% of the average wage. An individual whose earnings were at or below average could thus expect a retirement income from these public plans equivalent to only about 39% of what she had been earning before age 65.

The most important pension reform for women retiring in the future, and one that is supported by the Canadian Advisory Council on the Status of Women and other women's groups, the labour movement, and retirees' organizations, is an increase in the level of C/QPP benefits. Most groups recommend a doubling of benefit levels, from the current 25% of covered earnings to 50%. Such a provision would give women a much better chance of maintaining a reasonable standard of living in retirement. Since the C/QPP also includes part-time workers, improving the benefit level would also help women who are employed part-time. As already seen, few part-time workers are likely to benefit from the proposals to allow them to join private pension plans, since the majority of women work in sectors where few employers provide pension plans, even for full-time workers.

A higher benefit level for C/QPP would, of course, mean higher contributions, over and above the increases already announced. It has been estimated that a contribution rate of between 8.2% and 11.6% of contributory earnings (the earnings base on which contributions are made) would be required by the year 2000.[20] Half of this would be paid by the employer and half by the employee, as it is now. These rates are considerably higher than the current contribution rate, but they are still significantly lower than contribution rates to public pension plans in some other countries where the elderly already form a higher proportion of the population than they do in Canada.

In 1979, for example, contribution rates to public pension plans in Austria were 19.5%; in Finland, approximately 18%; in Germany, 18%; in Italy 23.5%; in the Netherlands, 20.75%; in Norway, 21.5%; and in Sweden, 20.5%.[21] However, the CPP reforms that took effect in 1987 did not include any proposals to increase the benefit level of the CPP. Consequently, it would appear that better pensions for women in the work force will depend on individuals making their own arrangements to save for retirement through such mechanisms as RRSPs. As already explained, this approach will do little to improve the incomes of women retiring in the future. There is thus a strong possibility that, unless further reforms are put in place, the majority of women who retire in the future will still have inadequate pensions, though not for the same reasons that make women's pensions inadequate today.

Benefits for Surviving Spouses

Providing better benefits for the surviving spouses of public and private pension plan contributors has been a major focus of pension reform as it relates to women. These benefits were originally designed to meet the needs of families where the husband is the breadwinner and the wife remains at home. Thirty or forty years ago, most families were of this type, and there was a need to ensure that a widow's pension income would continue when her husband died. Such benefits assumed a wife would be financially dependent on her husband, they were set at a certain percentage of her husband's earnings, and were usually discontinued if she married again. (This provision has only just been changed in the CPP.)

In most families today, however, both spouses are likely to have paid employment and both may have accumulated pensions in their own names, whether through the public system or through private arrangements. The rationale for survivor benefits now seems open to question. Some women's groups have suggested that surviving-spouse benefits in the C/QPP be abolished because they reinforce the notion that a wife is dependent on her husband (although benefits are available to either widows or widowers of contributors). Ironically, the same groups have recommended that survivor benefits be mandatory for private pension plans.

Abolishing survivor benefits completely could cause hardship, particularly because women's earnings are so much lower than men's. Even where a woman pensioner had her own retirement income, it would probably be much lower than that of her husband. Without survivor benefits, a wife who survived her husband would be in a much poorer financial situation than a husband who survived his wife.

Some of those involved in the pension debate have developed a new rationale for survivor benefits that is perhaps more in tune with present-day reality and changing family structure. It is based on the concept of marriage as a partnership of equals. The retirement income received by a couple, regardless of whether both were in the paid labour force, can be thought of as income to which they both contributed. When one spouse dies, the survivor is therefore entitled to maintain a certain standard of living relative to that enjoyed by the couple when both were alive. The principle would be that the surviving spouse's benefit should replace a certain percentage of the retirement income being received by the couple before the first spouse died, in the same way that the earnings-related pension received by a retiring contributor replaces a percentage of the pre-retirement income, so that a certain standard of living can be maintained.

Obviously there are some difficulties with this approach. For instance, the surviving spouse of a two-earner couple would be entitled to a larger benefit than would an individual with the same pre-retirement

150

earnings who had never married. In effect, survivor benefits provide a subsidy to married persons, although they do pay higher contributions. But since other social security and taxation measures also favour married people, this recognition of the institution of marriage might be justified. There is also the possibility, of course, that programs that discriminate in favour of married persons could be challenged under the Charter of Rights and Freedoms, but so far, this possibility does not seem to have been raised.

Pension reforms now being considered would make survivor benefits mandatory under private pension plans, unless both spouses agree in writing that they do not want this provision. Benefits for the surviving spouse would generally have to be at least 60% of the pension being paid to the contributor before s/he died.

Under the C/QPP, the surviving spouse of a contributor receives a benefit equivalent to 60% of the deceased contributor's pension, although if the survivor is under the age of 65, benefits are determined according to some rather complex rules and regulations. If the surviving spouse is already receiving a retirement pension from the plan, the combined benefit may not exceed the maximum retirement benefit. Common-law spouses may be entitled to survivor benefits, and the definition of common-law relationships has been made less restrictive in the recent reform of the CPP. The requirements now specify a "conjugal relationship with a person of the opposite sex", living together for at least one year, and cohabitation immediately prior to the death of the contributor.

Under the new amendments to the CPP, survivor benefits will no longer terminate on remarriage, and more generous rules will apply to the calculation of benefits where the surviving spouse already has a retirement pension (but the maximum benefit for the combined pensions will remain the same).

Pensions and Divorce

What happens to pension entitlements at divorce is a particularly important issue for women. Although matrimonial property laws in all jurisdictions now provide for assets to be divided between divorcing spouses on their request, only a few provinces specifically include pensions in the division of property. In most cases, it is up to the courts to decide whether a spouse is entitled to a share of the other spouse's pension. For many couples, accumulated contributions in a pension plan may be a substantial part of the assets of the marriage, and for women who have not worked outside the home, access to a spouse's pension may be an important protection for her retirement years.

As far as private pension plans are concerned, where judges decide that a wife is entitled to share her husband's pension, husbands may sometimes meet that obligation by transferring a sum equal to the present value of the pension that would eventually be received by the husband-contributor. This lump sum may then be placed in a locked-in account, such as an RRSP (except that amounts could not be withdrawn before retirement age), to provide a pension when the wife reaches retirement age. Alternatively, the husband (assuming he is the spouse who has a pension entitlement) may agree to pay a portion of his pension to his former wife, once he starts to receive it at retirement. It is important to note that the question of whether a spouse is entitled to a share of the other spouse's pension is governed by the matrimonial property laws of the province where the divorce takes place. Once it has been decided that a spouse is entitled to a share of the pension, the question of whether a particular pension plan can actually pay benefits to a non-contributor, and how this could be done, is governed by the pension legislation of the province or territory concerned. The question is further complicated by the fact that not all jurisdictions have pension benefits legislation. In these cases, the regulations of the particular pension plan may determine whether the non-contributor spouse can get the benefit to which the court has said she is entitled.

To date, Manitoba is the only province to specify in its pension benefits legislation that pension plans under its jurisdiction must pay half the value of a divorcing spouse's pension entitlement to the non-contributor spouse. The present value of the pension that will eventually be received must be estimated and that amount placed in a locked-in account to provide a benefit for the non-contributor spouse at retirement. In other provinces, the method of dividing a pension that courts have deemed must be shared has not yet been laid down in pension benefits legislation.

The federal *Pension Benefits Standards Act*, which regulates private pension plans under federal jurisdiction, such as those of banks and transportation and communications companies, allows pension plans to provide for a division of pensions if the divorcing spouses wish it. The rules also apply to common-law spouses, although there are few provinces where matrimonial property laws apply to common-law unions. Although a pension plan under federal jurisdiction can technically divide the pension entitlement of a contributor with her/his common-law spouse, most jurisdictions do not give such spouses the right to share in assets on the dissolution of a common-law union.

Under the C/QPP, spouses have been entitled since 1978 to apply for a division of pension credits at divorce. However, few have taken advantage of the provision, and the legal position has been confusing. It would appear that some women have agreed to waive any claim to a former husband's C/QPP benefits, in exchange for other financial considerations at the time of divorce. A subsequent application for a share in the C/QPP credits could not then be granted. The recent amendments to the CPP provide for mandatory division on divorce of CPP pension entitlements built up during the marriage by both spouses. Unlike the former provisions, where application had to be made within three years of the divorce, there is no time limit under the new legislation. As soon as the Minister of National Health and Welfare receives the necessary information, pension credits will be divided. However, if both spouses specifically surrender their claim to the CPP credits of the other, this agreement is binding on the Minister.

Homemaker Benefits

Much of the debate about women and pension reform has been taken up by the discussion of how best to provide pension income for women who have spent most of their adult lives as full-time homemakers. Although homemakers do receive pension income in their own names from the first tier of the existing system, many women feel the existing provisions do not adequately recognize the contribution made by women who work in their homes. It has been argued that because homemaking services undoubtedly have some value, they should be recognized explicitly by including full-time homemakers in the C/QPP. As we saw earlier, these plans are part of the second tier of the retirement income system, designed to provide a replacement income once an employee ends paid employment, and to preserve a certain standard of living for the retiree.

Given that homemakers have no income to be replaced, how could they be included in an earnings-related plan? The mechanism suggested is one where the homemaker's services would be assumed to have a certain monetary value, perhaps half the average wage. Contributions to the C/QPP would be based on this assumed income, and retirement benefits would be paid accordingly. Contributions would be made on behalf of the homemaker by "those who benefit from her services". The proposal assumes, in effect, that the homemaker is working for her husband and that, generally, he would have to contribute to the plan on her behalf, except in low-income families. In these cases, all other plan contributors would bear the cost of providing benefits to the full-time homemaker.

Groups supporting this proposal argue that the value of women's work in the home must be acknowledged specifically in this way and that such provisions are necessary to ensure that women who spend most of their lives as homemakers are not penalized by the retirement income system, as they are now. However, the proposals have raised a good deal of controversy, and a number of difficulties are immediately apparent:

■ If housework has an economic value that must be recognized by granting an earnings-related pension, what about the housework that is done by women who are also employed in the paid labour force? The

153

homemaker pension proposals suggest that only those women who remain largely or entirely outside the labour force do housework that has an economic value, while those in paid employment do not.

- The proposals assume that any woman who is not in paid employment is in fact a homemaker. Thus, a woman who is married to a high-income earner and is able to hire someone else to do her housework would still be defined as a homemaker entitled to a benefit from the C/QPP.

- The assumption that homemaking services draw a form of non-money income that must be replaced by a stream of money income when the homemaker reaches the age of 65 implies that the homemaking services cease at that point.

- A homemaker who receives no pay for her services up until the age of 65 is dependent on her husband's income, yet it is claimed she should not have to be dependent on his pension.

- If survivor benefits are demeaning because they reinforce dependency, does it not also imply dependency to have to rely on the husband to contribute to a homemaker pension?

The obvious problems associated with this proposal for homemaker benefits have led to heated debate and to rejection of the special homemaker contribution by a number of women's groups, by the labour movement and by anti-poverty and welfare organizations. These groups advocate a different approach to recognizing the contribution of full-time homemakers, giving them a pension in their own right but avoiding the inequities associated with the special benefit proposals. Instead of treating the wife as an employee of her husband or family, this approach is based on recognition of marriage as a partnership of equals. Pensions built up by the spouses during the marriage (in one-earner couples, this would mean the breadwinner spouse's pension entitlement) would be divided between the spouses when both reach retirement age. This would give a homemaker spouse a pension cheque in her own name, in recognition of her equal contribution to the marriage partnership.

It must be emphasized that women's groups advocating the special homemaker benefit also support the sharing of pension entitlements. The position thus has some unintended side-effects. The special homemaker benefit would not, in fact, provide a personal pension for the homemaker spouse, since it would have to be shared with her husband, just as he would have to share his pension entitlement with her. Ultimately then, the homemaker pension, as it is currently proposed, would be a special bonus to couples where only one of the spouses is in the paid labour force. As a result, a one-earner couple with pre-retirement earnings at the average wage, for instance, would be entitled to significantly larger benefits than a two-earner couple with the same pre-retirement earnings; this is because

154

the latter couple would not qualify for the homemaker benefit if both spouses earn half the yearly maximum insurable earnings or more. For the same reason, surviving spouses of one-earner couples would also be entitled to better pensions than surviving spouses of two-earner couples or single individuals in the same circumstances. Even though advocates of special benefits for homemakers propose abolishing survivor benefits, a spouse in a one-earner couple, entitled to the proposed homemaker benefit, would have a larger personal pension than would the surviving spouse in a two-earner couple where the family earnings are the same.

Critics of the proposed special benefit for full-time homemakers also raise more serious philosophical objections. By emphasizing additional benefits for the one-earner family (which is not the norm in Canada), at the expense of the two-earner family, it is felt that the proposals reinforce the traditional role of women. Those who continue to play that traditional role will be rewarded for doing so, while the majority of women, who must now work for pay in order to support their families, will be expected to fend for themselves. In other words, state support and encouragement is to be concentrated on the so-called traditional family. Such an emphasis, it is argued, sets up barriers that will prevent policy development more appropriate to the needs of today and, more particularly, to the needs of the future. Since no concrete proposals have been introduced to improve the retirement incomes of the women who spend most of their pre-retirement years in the work force, the needs of this majority of women will still not be met.

There is, however, a model for pension reform that would meet the needs of all women, regardless of their lifetime work pattern. It would recognize the contribution of homemakers and would ensure that they have adequate retirement incomes without favouring women who remain outside the work force over those who have paid employment. This model is the subject of the next section.

A Proposal to Benefit All Women

It has been generally agreed that the most important single pension reform for women is the doubling of benefit levels in the C/QPP. Such a measure would ensure that women in the paid labour force who have no private source of retirement income would receive decent pensions in retirement. But this proposal would also greatly benefit women who do not participate in paid employment. If they were given a right to share in their husbands' pensions once they reach retirement age, and if his C/QPP benefit were doubled, there would be a reasonable pension to be shared between the spouses. The homemaker spouse would receive a pension cheque in her own name at retirement, in recognition of her equal contribution to the marriage partnership. In addition, if her husband died, she could receive a proportion of his share of the joint pension, as a survivor benefit, to add to her own share. This combination of sharing and survivor benefits would provide adequate pensions for women in all circumstances. In fact, it has been estimated that widows who have not worked outside the home would get better pensions under this reform model than they would under the homemaker contribution model proposed by the Parliamentary Task Force on Pension Reform.[22] This is the reform model favoured by the Canadian Advisory Council on the Status of Women and other women's groups, by the labour movement, and by anti-poverty and welfare organizations.

The recent changes to the CPP did, in fact, provide for sharing pension entitlements between spouses by allowing either spouse in a continuing marriage or common-law relationship to apply on retirement to share the CPP pensions earned by both spouses during their marriage, provided they are both at least 60 years of age and have applied for any retirement pensions to which they are entitled under the plan. But the sharing will be voluntary, and the shared benefits will apply only while both spouses are alive. Once the first spouse dies, the survivor benefit will be based on retirement benefits that were payable to each spouse prior to sharing.

CONCLUSION

It is clear that the best hope that women have for adequate pensions in retirement will come through reform of public pension plans in the first two tiers of the retirement income system. Changes to the CPP have already been enacted, but they provide only a minimal improvement as far as women are concerned. The major issue — a higher benefit level for the C/QPP — has still not been addressed. Without this kind of change, the majority of women may still end up poor in old age.

NOTES

1. Canada, Statistics Canada, *The Labour Force* (Ottawa: Supply and Services Canada, 1985), catalogue no. 71-001, table 55.

2. Canada, Statistics Canada, *Income Distributions by Size in Canada* (Ottawa: Supply and Services Canada, 1984), table 67.

3. *Ibid.*, text table II.

4. *Ibid.*, text table IV.

5. *Ibid.*, table 67.

6. Census data for 1941 cited in Patricia Connelly, *Last Hired, First Fired: Women and the Canadian Work Force* (Toronto: The Women's Educational Press, 1978), table 1.1, p. 84.

7. Canada, Statistics Canada, *The Labour Force*, table 56.

8. *Ibid.*

9. National Council of Welfare, *1985 Poverty Levels* (Ottawa: 1985). Updated to 1986 by assuming an inflation factor of 4.2% for 1986.

10. Canada, Statistics Canada, *Income Distributions by Size in Canada*, table 67.

11. National Council of Welfare, *A Pension Primer* (Ottawa: 1984), p. 12.

12. Canada, Statistics Canada, unpublished data.

13. Canada, Statistics Canada, *The Labour Force*, table 80.

14. Canada, Department of Finance, *Building Better Pensions for Canadians* (Ottawa: Supply and Services Canada, 1984), p. 6.

15. Canada, Department of Finance, *Analysis of Federal Tax Expenditures for Individuals* (Ottawa: Supply and Services Canada, 1981), p. 19.

16. Canada, Department of Finance, *Building Better Pensions for Canadians*, p. 22.

17. National Council of Welfare, *A Pension Primer*, p. 61.

18. Canada, Statistics Canada, *Women in Canada: A Statistical Report* (Ottawa: Supply and Services Canada, 1985), table 15, p. 76.

19. *Ibid.*, table 14, p. 76.

20. Canadian Labour Congress, *The CLC Proposal for Pension Reform* (Ottawa: 1982), p. 118.

21. *Ibid.*, pp. 129-130.

22. National Council of Welfare, *Better Pensions for Homemakers* (Ottawa: 1984), p. 43.

CHAPTER TEN

FINANCIAL SECURITY IN RETIREMENT

Financial security during their retirement is of great concern to Canadian women, and rightly so. In recent years, they have decried their situation and, in particular, the poverty to which they are confined by the workings of the current retirement income security system. Their demands have even succeeded in stirring the various levels of government. A succession of task forces, study groups, parliamentary committees, and papers of various colours have been devoted to the status of the elderly, with most giving special attention to the status of retired women.

The objective of this chapter is to take stock of the question. The first section examines several notions essential to understanding the issues surrounding retirement problems. These include the uncertainty of the future and the differences between a retirement system based on savings and one based on transfer payments. Following a brief historical review, the current status of the retirement income protection system is considered. The major deficiencies in the system are identified and government action in recent years is noted. After a review of current proposals for improving public pension plans, the analysis is completed by discussing the proposals that respond specifically to the needs of women. Finally, some of the issues relating to the cost of reform are discussed.

UNDERSTANDING RETIREMENT ISSUES

Retirement is an event associated with a specific time of life. For some people, the event is still far off in the future, while for others, it is in the near future. In formulating retirement policies, however, it must not be forgotten that we are talking about the future. Because of this, policy-makers must bear in mind that the future is uncertain, and the implications of that uncertainty must be assessed. This in turn underlines the distinction between financing retirement through savings and financing retirement by means of transfer payments.

The Future is Uncertain

Because the future is uncertain, it is difficult to say what level of income will be necessary for retirement in 10, 20, or 40 years from now, and it is almost impossible to be certain of having saved enough money for retirement.

There are many sources of this uncertainty, but they can be divided into three major categories: changes in prices, changes in standards of living, and changes in one's personal status. These three sources of uncertainty are examined in order to identify their impact on retirement.

- Changes in prices

To determine the level of income necessary for retirement, the cost of the following goods and services must be determined:

- housing, whether rented or owned,

- food, clothing, utilities, and insurance,

- transportation (automobile, gasoline, public transit), and

- leisure activities (travel, television, theatre, books, social activities, sports, new consumer goods).

A review of changes in consumer prices since 1961 shows that the rate of price increases has not been constant throughout the period. Until 1972, prices increased only slightly; from 1972 to 1982, they increased almost 9% per year; between 1982 and 1985, prices went up by about 6% per year. Over the whole period, the average increase in prices was 6% per year. This means that what cost $100 in 1960 cost more than $400 in 1985.

When we look only at the past, it is clear what the increase in prices has meant. But when it comes to the future, there is a tendency to forget the magnitude of the problem. Advertisements for registered retirement savings plans (RRSPs) are a good example of this. Some claim that you can become a millionaire by putting a certain amount of money into a particular RRSP each year, but they fail to mention the future purchasing power of these savings. Let us look more closely at an example.

Consider the case of a 25-year-old woman earning $11,000 per year in 1985. This income level is about one-half the average salary in Quebec and is often suggested as a base for determining pension entitlement for homemakers.[1] If a woman contributes $220 each year to a pension plan (2% of her income of $11,000), at age 65 she will be entitled to a pension of $5,640 per year if her savings generate returns of 7% per year. Relative to an income of $11,000, a pension of $5,600 sounds good, but what will $5,600 be able to buy in 40 years' time?

Interest rates and price increases are linked. Interest rates are higher when prices go up quickly. If we assume that our savings are going to generate an average return of 7% per year over 40 years, we cannot assume that prices are going to stay constant over the same period.

160

Even if there is no direct relationship between the rate of inflation and interest rates, we can still say that, over a long period, the interest rate is about equal to the inflation rate plus the rate of increase in productivity. If capital accumulates at a rate of 7% per year, we can assume that prices will have increased by about 5.5% per year and productivity by 1.5%. An annual income of $11,000 today would be the equivalent of an income of $88,764 40 years from now.

In this example, going from an income of $11,000 to $88,700 over a period of 40 years makes the woman no richer. Society as a whole, however, is richer. To keep up with the increase in national wealth, income would also have to increase by about 7% per year, which would put it at about $154,000. Thus, a pension of $5,640 per year — the amount payable if $220 per year is set aside over 40 years—would be virtually worthless if annual incomes reached $154,000.

- Changes in living standards

In planning for retirement, should increases in the standard of living be taken into account? Is this asking too much of our retirement system?

Let us start by looking at how the standard of living has risen over the last 40 years. The period between 1945 and 1985 has seen:

- new products: radio, television, colour television, tape recorders, sound systems, microwave ovens, electric coffee-makers, modern heating systems, microcomputers, and so on;

- products available to a greater number of people: automobiles, air travel, annual vacations, telephones, washers and dryers, fresh fruit and vegetables in winter;

- improvements in old products: stoves, refrigerators, new clothing fabrics, boots, shoes, furniture; and

- more leisure time: shorter work days, shorter work weeks, longer annual vacations, more holidays.

Should people who are 65 years old today be satisfied with the standard of living they had 40 years ago? Certainly not. The lifestyle of 40 years ago no longer exists. But what will the standard of living be 40 years from now? What level of income will be necessary if retirees are to have a standard of living similar to the rest of society? Retirement planning must address these questions. To achieve a retirement policy worthy of the name, we must ensure that pensioners' disposable income after retirement will allow them to fit into the society of the day.

■ Changes in personal status

The two preceding sections illustrated the difficulty of determining, in advance, the level of income that will be necessary to provide a decent retirement in 40 years' time. This holds true for society as a whole. There is, however, another source of uncertainty that affects each of us differently. It has to do with changes in our personal status between now and the time of retirement and even during retirement. This uncertainty involves our ability to save between now and retirement, the particular conditions surrounding the date of retirement, and the lifestyle that we want to or will have to adopt at that time.

The uncertainty surrounding the ability to save for retirement is related principally to changes in economic status between now and then. Will there be economic crises, as in 1982, when real salaries decreased and almost 15% of the labour force was unemployed? Will savings have to be used to maintain our standard of living? Will we lose our savings because of bankruptcy or a successful lawsuit against us? If any of these situations were to occur, we would obviously be left with reduced savings upon retirement.

Apart from these economic possibilities, specific personal situations may force us to use our savings before the age of 65. A prolonged illness, whether our own or that of a family member, may make it necessary to spend our savings. Our children may have special needs that require unanticipated expenditures—the cost of an education away from home, for example, or the development of musical talents or athletic abilities. We may be the victim of an accident or an event that is not covered fully by insurance (fire, theft, auto accidents). Finally, change in the family situation (separation, divorce, death of a spouse, permanent disability of a family member) can radically affect material living conditions.

These events are not just the product of an overactive imagination; they occur regularly to Canadians at all income levels. They call into question the effectiveness of a retirement policy based essentially on private savings.

Savings vs. Transfer Payments

A retirement policy based on savings implies that everyone is responsible for accumulating, during their working years, the resources they will need for retirement. In other words, pensioners will be able to enjoy the benefits only of what they have set aside.

162

A retirement policy based on transfer payments, on the other hand, means that the incomes of pensioners are financed out of the incomes of those who are working. During their working years, workers set aside part of their incomes not for their own retirement, but to finance pensions for current pensioners. When it is their turn to retire, it will be the responsibility of those then working to finance them.

Obviously, no retirement system is based solely on one strategy. The current policy respecting financial security for retirement contains elements of both savings and transfer payments. Old Age Security and the Guaranteed Income Supplement are income transfers: they are financed out of the government's general revenues each year. Transfer payments also figure heavily in the Canada Pension Plan (CPP) and the Quebec Pension Plan (QPP), even though the benefits paid during retirement depend on the contributions made by recipients during their working years. On the other hand, employer-sponsored pension plans, registered retirement savings plans, personal savings, and private investments (the purchase of a house, for example) are sources of retirement income that depend on savings: they provide income to pensioners that varies depending on what has been put into them.

■ Private plans and pre-funding

It is perhaps useful to explain why employer plans must be based on savings while this is not necessarily the case with government plans. The basic reason lies in the fact that there is no guarantee that a company will still be in business in the future, while it is certain that there will always be a government. This permanence allows the government to base the financing of pension plans on the principle of reciprocity between generations of workers, which is impossible for private businesses.

Because it is not known whether private businesses will be there when it comes time to pay the pensions they have promised to their workers, they are required to set aside the amount of money now that will be necessary to cover that promise of future payment. This is known as the capitalization or pre-funding of a plan. It is a legal obligation for all occupational pension plans in which workers participate.

How does it work in real life? The main implication of pre-funding is that the cost of the pension plan must be calculated. This means establishing exactly what has been promised and how much it will cost to fulfil that promise. Let us take an example: an employer promises to pay workers, throughout their retirement, a pension of $15 per month for each year of service (during which they contributed to the plan). That is the promise. The cost of the promise depends on a number of factors: the retirement period and the cost of benefits, the role of interest in the cost of benefits, and pre-payment and the improvement of benefits.

163

The retirement period and the cost of benefits: The first factor is the retirement period: at what age will workers retire and at what average age will they die? The answer to the first question is normally found in the terms and conditions of a plan. A plan might provide the option of retirement at age 60, at age 65, or perhaps after 30 years of service. The answer to the second question is based on experience. The information is found in the mortality tables produced by statisticians and actuaries. These tables tell us that men have a life expectancy of roughly 70 years at birth and women, 78 years. The retirement period, that is, the period during which pension benefits must be paid, will therefore be longer for women than men. Actuaries can confirm that a promise to pay benefits costs more if it is made to women than if it is made to men.

The laws prohibiting discrimination on the grounds of sex have always had some difficulty dealing with the effect of the greater longevity of women on the cost of retirement plans. Until very recently, the general rule was that provisions based on actuarial principles (in other words, based on statistics) were not considered discriminatory and therefore illegal. The federal government has recently passed a new law, however, respecting occupational pension plans; it contains a provision prohibiting taking into account the sex of a participant in determining his or her contributions or even the benefits to which he or she will be entitled.[2] This responds to the repeated demands of women's groups, including the Canadian Advisory Council on the Status of Women.[3] How this provision will be applied in practice remains uncertain in the case of groups composed almost totally of one sex or the other.

The role of interest in the cost of benefits: Another factor determining the cost of the promise of pension benefits is the age of workers to whom promises are made. For example, the promise to pay benefits of $15 per month to a 20-year-old worker will materialize only in about 40 years. Between now and then, the money set aside will earn interest that can be used to pay part of the benefits. The cost of the promise is therefore reduced by that amount. On the other hand, if the worker is already 60 years old, a higher amount must be set aside now to cover the same obligations, because accumulated interest cannot be relied upon to finance much of the promise. The cost of an occupational pension plan will therefore depend on the average age of the group of workers to whom it applies as well as on interest rates.

Because the future is uncertain and it is not known exactly what will happen to interest rates between now and the time when benefits have to be paid, theories must be developed. This is what actuaries do. They have developed rules that allow them to construct a set of coherent, interrelated theories. Based on these actuarial assumptions, which are verified by the

164

various government agencies responsible for monitoring occupational plans, the costs of private pension plans can be determined.

Pre-payment and the improvement of benefits: The process of setting aside money now to cover the future cost of promised pension benefits affects the ability of private plans to move quickly to improve the status of elderly workers. When a new plan is started, for example, it will take 30 or 35 years before it begins to pay good benefits, that is, benefits as good as those promised to workers with many years of service. This is because it is necessary to set the money aside before the pension benefits can be paid.

■ Public pension plans and transfer payments

This last point is probably the most important difference between plans based on savings and plans based on transfer payments. Old Age Security (OAS) is certainly the purest transfer payment plan in the area of retirement. OAS represents a commitment by society as a whole to people age 65 and older, to pay a monthly pension of a certain amount, with specific indexing provisions, independent of the financial status of the recipient, and, most important, independent of any contribution they might have made in the past to financing the plan. Moreover, the pensions are paid out of current taxes. There is no money set aside to ensure that the plan will continue. OAS is not based on savings (money set aside) but on inter-generational reciprocity—on the promise that the system will still be in place when the workers of today reach the age of 65.

The Canada Pension Plan and Quebec Pension Plan reserves: The Canada Pension Plan and the Quebec Pension Plan (C/QPP) are also based on reciprocity and transfer payments, even though money is, in fact, set aside for them. The plans are based on transfer payments, however, because the level of contributions is not based strictly on the cost of delivering promised benefits as is the case with occupational plans.

The philosophy behind the C/QPP is different from that of Old Age Security in the sense that the C/QPP are not intended to pay identical benefits to all persons over 65 years of age, but rather to replace part of their employment income. As benefits are a function of previous salaries, the calculation of contributions is also based on salary. The contribution rate is currently fixed at 3.8% of salary[4] and is divided equally between workers and their employers. The purpose of this rate is not to pre-pay the plan—that is, to ensure that there will be enough money set aside to pay the promised benefits—but to smooth out the effects of demographics. To avoid sudden jumps in contribution rates, the new formula, in effect since January 1987, provides for a review of the rate every five years, with changes as appropriate to ensure that the reserves always correspond to the equivalent of at least two years of benefits. The C/QPP reserves therefore play a very different role than is the case with private plans.

It is for that reason that the C/QPP have been able to pay maximum pensions within just 10 years of their introduction. The first pensioners to receive the maximum pension had contributed for only 10 years, while the period of contribution would normally extend over almost 40 years — from the age of 18 to the age of retirement. These pensions were therefore financed by other workers, because workers who retired in the early years of the C/QPP's operation drew more out of the plan than they had put in. As these plans replace a portion of a pensioner's previous employment income, C/QPP benefits also represent transfers between people earning salaries.

Differences between the public plans and group insurance: Because the CPP and the QPP are based on contributions deducted from salaries and pay out different benefits depending on the pensioner's employment history, many people consider these plans to be like large group plans, similar to those of private employers. It is true that in both cases there is a major element of insurance, that is, a pooling of risk; the risks relate to a recipient living longer than average and therefore needing pension income for a longer than average period. This is what makes employer group plans (occupational pension plans) more attractive than the individual plans (RRSPs). But the public plans are more than group insurance plans. They are also social insurance plans because they may result in transfer payments.

Only governments can establish plans based wholly or partially on transfer payments, because only governments enjoy the necessary permanence to promise the workers of today that the same rules of the game will apply when they retire. The current contributions paid into the C/QPP are therefore used to pay the pensions of current pensioners and not to build up capital to pay future pensions. If homemakers were to contribute to public plans, they would participate in financing current pensioners while they themselves have no income of their own. It is analogous to requiring them to pay taxes today, while they have no income, in order to be entitled to receive Old Age Security later on.

RETIREMENT INCOME SECURITY: HISTORICAL PERSPECTIVE

The problems of retirement have taken on new dimensions since the development of the wage system, that is, since the standard of living of the vast majority of the population has depended on earning wages or a salary. This shift coincided with the industrialization of the economy.

166

The Self-sufficient Family

In the days when families were relatively self-sufficient, producing most of what they needed themselves, it was within families that the rules for sharing the benefits of production were decided. In addition, the family was legally obligated to look after all its members. Individuals who could not count on this family support (because they no longer had any family or because they were new immigrants) had to resort to public charity to survive. This kind of income security arrangement was viable as long as families were able to control their own production and not too many individuals had to resort to public charity.

With the advent of industrialization and the spread of wage and salary systems, these conditions changed. In losing control of their production, families also lost the ability to provide for the financial security of their members. Suddenly, their standard of living became dependent upon receiving monetary income, a salary. Any event that interrupted the family's income rendered it economically dependent on the rest of society; these events might include illness of the chief breadwinner of the family, unemployment, premature death, or loss of employment because of age. From that point on, it was illusory to think that families, no matter how carefully they planned, could shelter themselves entirely from economic risks. As time went by, society therefore developed a set of income security programs adapted to an economy based on paid employment.

The Welfare State and Prevailing Values

The gradual implementation of these programs was in keeping with certain values considered important by society at the time. These values are still fundamental to our social security system. One is the importance attached to individual responsibility. Programs were designed based on the conviction that it is primarily through their own work that people should provide for their needs. Program designers therefore took great pains to ensure that they did not encourage idleness and did not give income to people who were capable of working. Accordingly, programs were more generous to those who had good reasons for not being able to participate in the labour market.

Among the first programs adopted were those to assist needy mothers and elderly people in need. In the latter case, it was age that constituted the good reason; in the former, it was sex. An additional objective of assistance to needy mothers was to discourage mothers from entering the labour market so that they could devote themselves to what was considered their proper task: taking care of their children. This was a clear reflection of the attitude of the times, whereby a woman was perceived as an economic dependant of her husband and, where the husband could no longer assume that role, as a dependant of the state. This dependent status resulted from the importance that salaries had assumed in determining the standard of living of families and from the exclusion of women from the labour market.

For a long time, the provisions of some plans reflected this ambivalence with respect to the role of women: provisions stipulating the payment of widow but not widower pensions, family insurance policies available only to male workers, the practically automatic classification of single-parent family heads as unemployable for purposes of social assistance. Women today object strongly to the attitude that the financial security of women depends on the presence of a husband, primarily because the programs resulting from this attitude do not serve them well and, indeed, often leave them in poverty because the structure of families is changing.

The Evolution of Financial Security for Retirement

■ Assistance for the very poor

The old age financial security system has evolved a great deal since its inception. When it began, in 1927, it was simply an assistance system, somewhat like today's social assistance, and was directed only to people over 70 years old who did not have the financial means to provide for their needs. It was based on a needs test. Starting in 1951, assistance was given selectively to people at age 65 and universally to everyone over age 70. It was eventually given to everyone starting at age 65. When it was granted on a universal basis, it lost its character as an assistance system and became what is now called Old Age Security.

■ Old Age Security

This program pays a uniform amount to everyone who satisfies the age requirements, regardless of their previous activities and financial status. Initially, this program had the responsibility of providing all Canadians with a level of income upon retirement that would put them above the poverty line. It is financed through current revenues of the federal government (that is, through taxes) and therefore constitutes income transfers between generations — those people with incomes finance pensions for persons 65 years of age and older.

■ The limitations of private savings

The history of the evolution of pensions tells us, however, that people do not simply want to be given a subsistence income upon retirement; they also want to maintain their standard of living. For a long time, the only means available to do this was private savings. The occupational pension plans implemented at the workplace were developed to help them achieve this objective. These plans have serious limitations, however. Only a minority of workers are actually covered by such plans; when workers change employers they can lose their entitlement to a pension;[5] and the requirement that private plans be pre-paid means waiting about 30 years before a plan's pension benefits are satisfactory. Finally, uncertainty about the future, especially about the increase in salaries and interest rates, means businesses often refuse to index their plans; thus the pensions paid out are often ridiculously low compared to what workers need to maintain their standard of living upon retirement. In addition, few private plans provide for the payment of benefits to a surviving spouse. This latter deficiency has been corrected, in the case of plans under federal jurisdiction, by passage of the *Pension Benefits Standards Act* in June 1986. The limited coverage of private plans and the absence of indexing continue to be limitations, however.

■ Canada and Quebec Pension Plans

It was not until 1966 that public employment-related pensions came into being, in the form of the Canada Pension Plan and the Quebec Pension Plan. The objective of the new plan was to replace a portion of a retiree's previous employment income upon retirement. However, the level of replacement is low —25%—and the insurable maximum is set at the level of the average industrial wage. Therefore, the maximum C/QPP payment available to any person is 25% of the average industrial wage. To become eligible for the C/QPP, it is necessary to contribute to the plan for one year, at or above the minimum pensionable earnings. In 1987, this minimum is $2,500 per year. Participation is mandatory for those who receive employment income. Unlike private plans, there is no coverage problem.

C/QPP pensions are indexed to the annual increase in the cost of living. The plan also provides for the payment of pension benefits to a surviving spouse and children, whether death occurs before or after retirement, provided that the deceased contributed to the plan for a certain number of years. The vesting period of the plan was established at 10 years. In other words, the plan paid out maximum benefits just 10 years after its commencement. The major deficiencies associated with private plans were therefore corrected. However, the poverty problems of the elderly remained; those who had already left the labour market were not entitled to a pension, and those who left before the end of the first 10 years were eligible for only a partial pension.

■ Guaranteed Income Supplement

The Guaranteed Income Supplement (GIS) was introduced in January 1967. Then, as now, the GIS was subject to an income test. It is reduced by $1 for each $2 of income received from another source, with the exception of income from Old Age Security. In the beginning, GIS was designed to be a transitional measure and was to supplement the incomes of those who had not had time to accumulate public pensions based on employment earnings. GIS did not disappear, however. On the contrary, it is now an even more important component of the whole retirement income scheme.

This is because the combination of Old Age Security and public pension plan benefits on its own is insufficient to keep pensioners above the poverty line. Old Age Security has not been fully indexed to the increase in the cost of living[6] and has certainly not kept up with the increase in average wages. While at one time it represented about 20% of the average industrial wage, it now represents only about 13%.[7] Rather than increasing OAS, successive governments have preferred to raise the level of the Guaranteed Income Supplement. Since this latter program is selective rather than universal, it costs less money to upgrade this program than to upgrade Old Age Security.

Summary

The situation today is a product of this historical evolution. A bare minimum income is provided by two programs, Old Age Security and the Guaranteed Income Supplement, while continuity with previous income is supposed to be achieved through the Canada and Quebec Pension Plans. However, the replacement levels of these two plans are so low that even persons drawing the maximum pension have to resort to the GIS if they have no other sources of income. Thus, the income security system in Canada still relies very heavily on individual responsibility and savings to provide a retirement income above the poverty line. We now look more specifically at the status of women in this system.

THE CURRENT STATUS OF WOMEN

Women, particularly single elderly women, are poor. To rectify this situation, specific changes to the income security system have been proposed in the past decade. Before examining the proposed solutions, let us look at the current status of women within the public plans.

As women's economic role is changing, a change that involves increasing participation by women in the labour market for longer and longer periods, it has become impossible to find a model to illustrate the status of the average woman. Women today are facing a wide range of

170

experiences and problems. Accordingly, several typical cases have been selected to help demonstrate the overall status of women with respect to income security, especially during retirement.

The different situations facing women are best illustrated using cases from different age groups. First, the status of women who have never participated in public plans will be considered; this allows an examination of retirement income levels for a couple that only receives one retirement pension. The example of women over 65 years of age is used, even though the situation is identical in the case of younger women who have never or rarely participated in the labour market.

Next, examining the case of women in their fifties allows us to look at the provisions of public plans that apply when the spouse dies before retirement age and when a couple separates or divorces.

Finally, when examining the case of young women, we make the reasonable assumption that they participate almost continuously in the labour market, with the exception of the years spent with their young children. Thus, the measures taken to account for the unique role of women in childbearing can be analyzed and the effects on retirement incomes of the disparities in the salaries of men and women can be highlighted.

Women Over 65 Who Have Never Had Paid Employment

This example illustrates clearly the philosophy of the public income security plans with respect to the treatment of women. These women conformed to what society expected of them. Their main occupation was to raise children and keep house while their husbands went about earning a living; put another way, these women participated, as unpaid workers, in the family enterprise. For their entire lives, they had no independent income. Their contribution to the welfare of their families was not monetary. In our society, however, standards of living depend directly on disposable monetary income. Society has relied implicitly on the existence of a system of private sharing, within the family, to deal with the problems of survival of these women. Once retirement age is reached, it is presumed that the system is still working. To the extent that both spouses are still alive, this is quite possibly the case. The problems arise after the death of the husband. Let us take the example of a fictitious couple whose retirement income consists of the following:

Two Old Age Security pensions	$ 6,960
Quebec Pension Plan (or CPP) pension	5,800
Occupational pension plan pension	3,000
Guaranteed Income Supplement	900
Total	**$16,660**

The poverty line for a couple in 1986 was estimated to be about $16,350 by the Senate Committee on Poverty and between $9,900 and $12,800, depending on where the couple lives, by Statistics Canada.[8] The couple in our example is therefore above the poverty line, but their situation cannot be fully understood unless we also have an idea of their pre-retirement income. As the QPP pension indicated corresponds to the maximum amount payable in 1986, we can infer that the husband's employment income was always equal to or greater than the insurable maximum, which was $25,800 in 1986. Let us suppose that this was in fact their income level. With a retirement income of $16,600, this couple is living on 65% of its previous income. The fact that they are receiving a pension of $3,000 from an occupational pension plan helps them reach a level of replacement income that is high enough to put them above the poverty line. But what happens if the husband dies? The financial status of his widow could well be as follows:

Old Age Security	$ 3,480
QPP or CPP surviving spouse pension	3,500
Occupational plan survivor's pension	0
Guaranteed Income Supplement	2,400
Total	**$ 9,380**

This example is typical. Upon the death of her spouse, a widow suffers a significant loss in income. Indeed, she finds herself below the poverty line for a single person — estimated at $9,800 in 1986 by the Senate Committee (and up to $9,700 by Statistics Canada). The fact that the occupational plan to which her husband contributed did not provide benefits for a surviving spouse is not the only reason for this dramatic drop in income. If the widow had received a survivor's pension from the occupational plan equal to 50% of her husband's retirement pension, her total income would have increased not by $1,500 but by only $750, because the Guaranteed Income Supplement would have been reduced by $750 under the rules of the program. She would still be very close to the poverty line.

This situation illustrates the two main deficiencies in Canada's retirement income security system. First, the total of the two universal plans is insufficient to guarantee an income above the poverty line in all circumstances. Second, the element responsible for maintaining income continuity — the Quebec Pension Plan or the Canada Pension Plan — is not fulfilling its role. Even before the death of the husband, this couple was barely above the poverty line, despite the fact that they had made a good average living throughout their working life.

Women in Their Fifties

This group of women illustrates the diversity of situations in which women find themselves today. One-third of them have paid employment. Their status in the labour market is not enviable, however. The kind of jobs they hold and the number of hours they work are such that their employment income is very low. In 1981, it was around $11,500, while the average income of men of the same age was $18,000. Most often, these women have spent some years at home raising their children. As a result, they have not contributed to retirement plans for most of their lives. Furthermore, this group of workers has the lowest rate of coverage by occupational pension plans, whether because plans exclude part-time workers or because companies do not have plans at all. Whether they participate in the labour market or work at home, these women are vulnerable to the effects of household disintegration, whether caused by separation, divorce, or the death of the spouse.

■ Death of the spouse before retirement age

The death of the husband, with its financial consequences for the family, is one of the main risks against which workers have long wanted to insure themselves. The development of life insurance, especially group insurance, is ample demonstration of this. Life insurance, however, normally pays a lump sum upon death; it is not sufficient to allow the survivor to live without another source of income. Occupational pension plans do not generally provide for the payment of benefits to the surviving spouse if the worker dies before reaching retirement age. Only the public plans cover this eventuality. The objective of providing income continuity is far from being reached, however.

The benefits payable to surviving spouses under the age of 65 is one of the points on which the Canada Pension Plan and the Quebec Pension Plan differ. The Quebec Pension Plan calls for a higher pension to be paid to the surviving spouse and a lower pension to the children. Quebec figures are used in this paper. It should be borne in mind, however, that the situation is that much worse in the rest of Canada.[9]

Survivor benefits are given without an income test. In our example, it is therefore assumed that the widow is a homemaker, without other independent income. The pension amounts would not change if she had a paying job.

The Quebec Pension Plan pays surviving spouse benefits that vary according to the age and family responsibilities of the survivor. Between the ages of 45 and 54, the pension is made up of a fixed amount, the same for everyone, together with a percentage (37.5%) of the retirement pension to which the deceased was entitled. Between the ages of 55 and 64, the same principle applies, but the fixed amount is higher by about $65 per month. Below the age of 35, if there are no dependent children, no pension is paid. If there is a dependent child, the pension is the same as for survivors over 45 years of age. If the deceased was entitled to the maximum pension (if his earned income had always been equal to or greater than the insurable maximum), the benefits for the surviving spouse would also be at the maximum and, in 1986, would bring in the following income:

Where there are dependent children	$4,988
Survivor between the ages of 45 and 54	$4,988
Survivor between the ages of 55 and 64	$5,770

For spouses between 35 and 44, the survivor's pension is calculated as a percentage of the pension paid at 45 years of age. That amount is reduced by 10% for each year remaining between the survivor's current age and the age of 45. For example, if the widow is 43 years old, she will receive 80% of $4,988. Recently, these pensions became payable even after remarriage.

Women in their fifties with no source of income other than the survivor's pension must resort to social assistance. Their situation is, nevertheless, better than that of people who depend entirely on social assistance. Because the survivor's pension is given without an income test and is therefore not reduced if income is received from other sources, surviving spouses can improve their financial status more easily than they could if all of their income came from social assistance.

Clearly, income levels offered by surviving spouse benefits are insufficient to provide income continuity upon the death of the spouse, despite the fact that this is the rationale for the existence of these benefits. In spite of these low levels, surviving spouse benefits represent 25% of all monies paid out by the QPP. Proposals for improving these benefits are therefore always complex, particularly because of the financial implications. We return to this question in the following section.

■   Separation or divorce

Separation and divorce can also trigger a dramatic drop in the income of a family. They also highlight the problems of basing income security programs on the theory that private income transfers occurring within the family should remain in the private sector and that the state should not interfere with them.

Without going into detail about the difficulties of enforcing maintenance orders (see Chapter Two), suffice it to say that women who find themselves at the head of a single-parent family have considerably increased chances of being poor. Income security programs do not really

174

make it possible for them to avoid poverty. Until retirement age, social assistance is available for women unable to re-enter the labour market. Certain tax measures (the equivalent-to-married exemption, taking the place of the married exemption) and certain provisions of specific programs (the subsidy for child-care expenses) have been implemented gradually to help rectify the extremely precarious situation of women heading single-parent families.

The effects of separation and divorce on retirement income are different. In the case of divorce, the marriage is dissolved, and there is no longer any contractual relationship between the ex-spouses. Therefore, there is no longer any entitlement to a survivor's pension for either spouse. Divorce may occur in a couple where responsibilities were split along traditional lines—where the woman stayed home to take care of her husband and children or contributed to the family enterprise without pay. During the time they lived together, it can be assumed that the principle of private sharing was followed, at least for day-to-day expenses. Upon the dissolution of this marriage, however, some find it difficult to extend the principle of sharing to all the assets accumulated during the period of cohabitation. Yet, the arrangement adopted by the couple while they lived together was satisfactory to them; the woman's contribution to the household increased the level of the family's welfare in non-monetary ways, in turn allowing the husband to accumulate financial assets more easily, including pension credits.

It was not until 1977 that the Quebec Pension Plan incorporated a provision allowing credit-splitting upon divorce for pension credits accumulated during the period of cohabitation. Splitting is not automatic; one of the spouses must request it within three years of the divorce. Since January 1, 1987, pension-splitting in cases of divorce has been automatic under the Canada Pension Plan.

The main effect of credit-splitting is to confirm that, during the years of cohabitation, even where the circumstances were such that the monetary income earned by each spouse was different, the accumulated pension credits belong equally to both spouses, since their purpose is to maintain income continuity upon retirement. The greater the disparity between the spouses' incomes, the more reasonable it is to believe that the couple had an implicit agreement to split monetary income and therefore also to share any benefits associated with that income. Pension credits are one of those benefits.

Under the credit-splitting rule, a woman who has stayed at home throughout her marriage can thus be credited with half the value of the C/QPP benefits her husband has accumulated over the same period. She will no longer be entitled to survivor benefits, but she will nevertheless share in the value of the pension. If the woman received salary income during the marriage, credit-splitting means that the average of the credits she and her

175

husband accumulated during the period will be hers. This mitigates the effects of her shorter length of participation in the labour market and her lower salary.

In the case of separation, nothing in the QPP at this time provides for splitting accumulated pension credits. In the CPP, splitting is possible, effective January 1987, if requested by one of the spouses. With separation, the spouses continue to be entitled, in principle, to survivor benefits. But as the plans also provide for the payment of benefits to surviving common-law spouses, it is possible for two spouses to claim survivor benefits. If, following separation, one of the spouses forms another couple there might be two surviving spouses. The plan provides for the payment of only one survivor's pension, however. Each case must then be examined on its merits by plan administrators. Generally speaking, the last spouse, that is, the common-law spouse, seems to be favoured. The recent amendment to the CPP to allow pension credit-splitting in the case of separation therefore rectifies a situation that often left the first spouse without entitlement. Unfortunately, the QPP has not yet been similarly amended.

Younger Women

Younger women are increasingly involved in the labour market. The problems they face on retirement, however, still resemble those of their elders; these problems arise from the fact that their employment income is generally lower than that of men and that they often have to leave the labour market temporarily to take care of young children.

■ The drop-out provision

Childrearing responsibilities are taken into account by the C/QPP provision allowing women to exclude from their contribution period the years when they had children under the age of seven. Known as the drop-out provision, this rule is important in calculating pension entitlements. Let us examine how it works.

The contribution period is the period during which people who receive employment income must contribute to the Quebec Pension Plan or the Canada Pension Plan. It ordinarily includes the period between the age of 18 (or the year 1966, the date the plans started) and the time when a pension becomes payable. The level of earnings received during the contribution period is compared to the plan's maximum insurable earnings to determine the amount of pension payable. By allowing women to exclude the years when they were taking care of their children, the C/QPP allow women to receive a pension based only on income received during the other years.

The provision is mainly to prevent women being penalized for withdrawing from the labour market while they had young children or for taking part-time, low-paying jobs during that period. The provision benefits women who later return to the labour market and earn higher salaries. For mothers who were never in the labour market or who do not return to the labour market, this measure has no effect, because they will not have any C/QPP pension in their own name.

- Effects of income disparities on retirement income

The definitive solution to the problem of the low salaries among women must be the elimination of income disparities. Women must continue to fight for greater equality in the labour market, through employment equity programs and demands for equal pay for work of equal value, to eliminate the problem at its source.

For the moment, however, these disparities exist and do affect retirement income. The problem is compounded by the increase in part-time employment. Since 1982, the majority of new jobs created in Quebec have been part-time jobs, and the vast majority of them are held by women. In Canada as a whole, 27.9% of new jobs were part-time jobs. The incomes on which retirement pensions will be calculated will therefore be lower, resulting in the further entrenchment of the income disparities between retired men and women.

In addition, the current method of calculating QPP pension for surviving spouses will continue to favour men. The system in effect offers a choice to surviving spouses over the age of 65. They may choose to continue to receive either their full retirement pension, together with 35% of the pension of their deceased spouse, or 60% of their own pension plus 60% of that of their spouse. In either case, the combined pension may not exceed the maximum pension that would be paid to a single pensioner.

Where the original pensions are unequal, it is better for the spouse who receives the higher pension to choose the first option (100% + 35%). This is normally the choice men would make. The spouse who receives a much lower pension than his/her spouse is better off choosing the second option (60% + 60%). In the most extreme case, where the husband is entitled to a maximum pension while the wife receives no pension of her own, the result depends on which one of the spouses dies. If the husband dies, the survivor's pension will be 60% of the pension the deceased was receiving (60% of the maximum pension and 60% of zero). If the situation is reversed, the husband will be entitled to keep his full pension (100% of the maximum pension and 35% of zero). Although the couple shared the same standard of living during the husband's working years, the QPP as it now stands creates a situation where only the woman suffers a drop in pension income upon the death of her spouse.

An amendment to the Canada Pension Plan in effect since the beginning of 1987 allows this situation to be corrected. For persons covered by the CPP, it is now possible for spouses to split pension benefits once both have reached retirement age. If splitting is requested, the two pensions will obviously be equal. The choice under the surviving spouse option will therefore be available on identical terms, no matter who survives.

DEFICIENCIES IN THE CURRENT SYSTEM

This brief review of the characteristics of the current system of retirement income security quickly reveals its major weaknesses. The analysis is facilitated by the fact that the dissatisfaction of pensioners has forced governments and other groups to take a hard look at their situation in recent years. Several government studies have been produced,[10] and lobby groups interested in the issue have analyzed the problem and submitted proposals for reform. Women's groups have been particularly active on the issues surrounding retirement because women are not well served by the current system. These groups have certainly succeeded in sensitizing the public to the need to attack the problem of poverty among retired women. These studies identify three deficiencies in the current system:

- The minimum income guaranteed by Old Age Security and the Guaranteed Income Supplement is insufficient. Their combined benefits do not guarantee the elderly an income above the poverty line. This shortcoming is particularly significant for single people.

- The Canada Pension Plan and the Quebec Pension Plan are not properly fulfilling their role of maintaining pre-retirement standards of living. The level of earnings replacement, set at 25% since the plans first came into effect, is clearly inadequate for reaching that objective.

- The C/QPP do not take satisfactory account of the sharing of responsibilities and income between spouses. Where the household arrangements are such that a woman spends more time at home and less time in the labour market than her husband, the plans create a situation where the husband receives a higher income on retirement. Women deplore not only the financial consequences of this situation but also the fact that the plans fail to recognize the social value of their role in raising children.

178

GOVERNMENT RESPONSES TO DATE

Governments have taken some steps with respect to the retirement income system since the problem of poverty among the elderly first began to receive public exposure. By looking at the measures adopted, we can infer how governments approach the problem and where they might look for solutions. The measures adopted recently deal with almost all components of Canada's income security system.

Old Age Security

The federal government made Old Age Security subject to the 6% (1983) and 5% (1984) programs, limiting the indexing of pensions. The Guaranteed Income Supplement was increased accordingly. The net effect is that OAS has lost its relative importance in the overall scheme of retirement income security. In the 1985 budget, the government proposed a permanent limitation on pension indexing, but as a result of pressure from seniors, they had to abandon this proposal soon after. Their objective was, however, the same as that of the 6% and 5% program, that is, to reduce the universal part of the retirement income security program (OAS) and make it up through the selective part, the Guaranteed Income Supplement.

Guaranteed Income Supplement

GIS is playing an increasingly important role in the overall scheme of retirement income. When it was introduced in 1967, it represented 40% of Old Age Security. By 1986, it had reached 77% of the value of OAS for couples and 119% for a single person. This is the result of a gradual adjustment leading to an escalation in the GIS for single persons. Indeed, all the studies had shown that single retired people were much further below the poverty line than couples, largely as a result of GIS rates being too low.

Canada Pension Plan and Quebec Pension Plan

Since 1984, both plans have eliminated the practice of stopping survivor benefits upon remarriage. This change reflects a shift in attitudes: there has been a progression from the concept of the survivor pension being a measure designed to aid economic dependants (read: female dependants) to a concept of the pension as a means of providing income continuity when a member of the family dies.

During the same period, the QPP increased survivor benefits to persons over age 55, to take into account the difficulty these people, particularly women, were having re-entering the labour market. At the same

179

time, rules were established to allow voluntary retirement at age 60 and to relax the eligibility criteria for disability pensions for those age 60 to 64. These last two measures were seen as a response to the extremely difficult conditions in the labour market and have been available to persons covered by the CPP since the beginning of 1987. These are in addition to the other CPP reforms mentioned earlier: automatic credit-splitting on divorce, voluntary credit-splitting on separation, and optional pension-splitting between spouses in a continuing marriage when both reach retirement age.

Personal Savings

It is undoubtedly in the area of personal savings that governments have legislated most actively. The federal government has proposed reforms to occupational pension plans that came into effect in January 1987. The reforms deal with certain major deficiencies in private plans: quicker vesting of pension entitlements, regardless of the worker's age; a requirement that employers assume half the pension costs; transferability of pension credits when a worker leaves his/her employer; improved coverage for part-time workers; an obligation to provide survivor benefits; prohibition of sex discrimination within the plans; and better information for plan participants. These reforms respond to certain criticisms that have been voiced about private plans. One major omission, however, is the indexing of these pensions.

The most important changes with respect to personal savings for retirement are tax amendments respecting the treatment of registered retirement savings plans. The amendments allow much higher deductions from taxable income for amounts placed in RRSPs by workers without occupational plans sponsored by employers. Through this measure, the government is agreeing to provide financial help for individuals to save for their retirement. The help is in the form of reduced taxes and is mainly beneficial to people with high incomes. Moreover, the effects on retirement income security are uncertain for three reasons: savings may be used for other purposes before retirement, the people most likely to be poor during retirement cannot take advantage of it, and the measure helps those who have always had the means to enjoy a decent retirement through their savings. The fact that governments have chosen to base their reforms on occupational plans and RRSPs, which are based on the principle of private savings, reflects a refusal to improve public plans, which are the only ones capable of improving the retirement income of the vast majority of Canadians within a relatively short period.

OPTIONS FOR REFORM

The specific problems of retired women—that is, poverty and the lack of recognition for their work in the home—can only be addressed through the

180

public plans. Indeed, in the earlier discussion about the differences between plans based on savings and plans based on transfer payments we concluded that any solution based on savings can only perpetuate in retirement the income disparities that exist during the working years. Furthermore, any solution based on personal savings will not produce improvements in the overall situation for some time to come. It must also be emphasized that very few women in the labour market are covered by private employer-sponsored plans, whether because they work part-time or because they work in industries where employers seldom have pension plans.

As for the public plans, if they are to provide a satisfactory solution to women's retirement income problems, they must first be improved for everyone. The major cause of poverty among women is that the public plans are generally inadequate for all recipients. The first step, therefore, must be to improve these plans.

Old Age Security and Guaranteed Income Supplement

Of all the proposals for reforming the retirement income security system, there is one on which everyone agrees: the level of guaranteed minimum income for the elderly must be increased at least to the point where pensioners will not be below the poverty line. This guaranteed income is currently provided for by Old Age Security and the Guaranteed Income Supplement. To minimize the costs of implementing this proposal, some suggest that only the GIS be increased. Others suggest that there also be an increase in Old Age Security so that it always represents at least half the guaranteed minimum income.

The Parliamentary Task Force on Pension Reform went further, suggesting that OAS be raised initially and that it be indexed in future to increases in the average wage rather than increases in prices. In this way, the standard of living provided by the pension would increase at the same rate as the average standard of living for society as a whole.

At the beginning of this chapter we noted the importance of predicting increases in the standard of living of pensioners. It would therefore appear that a mechanism such as indexing Old Age Security to increases in the average wage is consistent with the objectives of a coherent retirement income security system. If this is not done, the income level provided for retirement will never be adequate to allow pensioners to participate as full members of society.

Canada Pension Plan and Quebec Pension Plan

The inability of these two plans to provide income continuity on retirement could be rectified by raising the rate of replacement of previous salaries.

The rate is currently fixed at 25%, with a ceiling at the level of the average industrial wage (about $25,800 in 1986). Several groups have suggested raising the replacement rate to 50%.[11] This improvement alone would considerably change the situation of pensioners and of everyone receiving survivor benefits, which also depend on the level of retirement pensions. At the 50% level, the maximum pensions in 1986 would have been as follows:

Retirement pension: 50% of $25,800	$12,900
Survivor pension at age 65	$ 7,740
Survivor pension between ages 55 and 64 (QPP)	$ 8,425
Survivor pension under age 55 (QPP)	$ 7,635
Survivor pension under age 65 (CPP)	$ 5,930

These new pensions would be added, where applicable, to Old Age Security benefits, which would also have increased. With this proposal, fewer pensioners would have to resort to GIS; this is consistent with the intent of the program, which is directed to a relatively small number of people whose pre-retirement income was low.

Other recommendations have also been made to improve the C/QPP. One recommendation is to reduce the number of contribution years required for entitlement to the maximum pension. Currently, every worker is allowed to eliminate from the contribution period the years when earnings were lowest, up to a maximum of 15% of the period, before calculating pension entitlements. Some have proposed that the maximum be raised to 25% or 30%.

Increasing the number of years that can be excluded from pension calculations would reduce the impact on retirement of any income interruptions experienced during a person's working years, for example, for educational leave, leave to upgrade skills, unemployment, or family responsibilities beyond the current drop-out period (taking care of children up to 7 years of age). Given that one of the differences between men and women is the number of years they spend in the labour market, such a measure would serve to reduce the disparity between the pensions paid to women and those paid to men. It would, however, benefit everyone. Indeed, it is surprising to discover that few workers actually qualify for the maximum pension, most often because of income interruptions rather than because their salaries were lower than the insurable maximum.

Another recommendation, proposed mainly by unions, is to increase the level of insurable earnings. At present, the C/QPP insure only that part of a worker's salary that is lower than the average industrial wage. This recommendation would fix the maximum insurable earnings at one and one-half times the average industrial wage. If this were the case, all incomes less than $35,000 would be insured by the public plans, and

182

there would no longer be any need to expand private plans for the vast majority of the population. The role of the private plans would be limited to dealing with specific provisions (such as retirement age) and to covering higher incomes.

Increasing the replacement rate of salaries to 50% and increasing the number of low-income years that can be deducted in calculating pensions are consistent with the current orientation of the retirement income security system, in that they leave room for private efforts and foresight. They are therefore more likely to be adopted. The results would be significant and would actually improve the situation of all pensioners. The financial status of retired women cannot be improved unless the public plans as a whole are improved.

WOMEN AND INCOME SECURITY

Women have undoubtedly been the most active group in voicing demands with respect to the retirement income security system. They have generally supported the proposals just outlined for increasing Old Age Security and the Guaranteed Income Supplement as well as upgrading the Canada Pension Plan and the Quebec Pension Plan.

Analyzing the causes of poverty among elderly women exposes other deficiencies in the retirement income system. These relate to provisions for income-splitting within the family and recognition of the value of work in the home. A number of possible solutions have been offered, some of which are complementary while others are incompatible with each other. These solution models can be grouped under three headings: the splitting of pension credits, the recognition of work at home, and the reform of benefits for surviving spouses.

Splitting Pension Credits

Splitting pension credits between members of a couple is probably the one major demand on which there has been unanimity. It already applies in the case of divorce—in Quebec upon the request of one of the spouses, and in the rest of Canada automatically since the beginning of 1987.

Advocates of reform believe this requirement should also cover pension credits accumulated in private plans. Under family laws in force in certain provinces, this measure is already in effect. Private plans under federal jurisdiction have been subject to this requirement since January 1, 1987. In the case of legal separation, some propose that there should be credit-splitting at the request of one of the spouses. The CPP now offers this option.

183

The rationale for splitting in the case of divorce—that is, recognition that pension credits are assets belonging jointly to both members of a couple—has now been extended to proposals respecting retirement more generally. Splitting would be done automatically when the younger spouse reaches retirement age. This would mean that when both spouses are retired, they would receive the same amount of pension. As outlined earlier, the CPP now allows this splitting on a voluntary basis.

By itself, this recommendation does not change a retired couple's income, but it does make the equal splitting of that income official. Since the two pensions would be equal, the survivor's pension would also be equal, regardless of whether the man or woman dies first. This issue is addressed later in this chapter.

This recommendation has the added advantage of demonstrating to everyone, not just women, the true value of the plan. If it were implemented today, for example, without other improvements in the plan, men would see it as a deterioration in the good pensions they now receive. Thus, it is in the interest of both men and women to upgrade the plan.

Credit-splitting does not, however, resolve the problem of the inadequacy of the pensions women accumulate in their own names. This problem, which is related to the lack of recognition of the social value of the work women do in the home and with children, has given rise to numerous proposals.

Recognition of Work in the Home

Women have been demanding greater financial independence for a long time. When it comes to retirement, this demand is related directly to the poverty imposed on elderly women by the current system. Several proposals to correct the situation have been made. The various demands are not all mutually compatible and do not always fit in at the same place in the overall income security system.

■ Exclusion of the years spent raising children

One proposal enjoys unanimous support. It has to do with recognizing that women (and men) who temporarily interrupt their paid work to care for children should not be penalized. Everyone supports the provision already in effect that excludes from the calculation of pension benefits the low-income years where there were children under the age of seven at home. Some would broaden this provision to encompass children up to the age of eleven as well the presence of a disabled person or invalid.

This measure benefits women who eventually return to the labour market. The exclusion of low-income years allows them to obtain a higher pension, calculated on the basis of the years of greatest participation in the labour market. This is possible only because they do return to the labour market and therefore have the higher-income years on which to base a calculation. The cost of this measure is currently shared by all contributors to the C/QPP.

■ Inclusion of the years spent raising young children

To provide additional C/QPP benefits and increase the retirement income of women who raise children but do not return to the labour market, numerous women's groups have proposed that pension credits be applied automatically to people who stay at home to raise their young children. These credits could be based on a notional salary equal to half the average industrial wage. While the children are under the age of seven, beneficiaries would not be required to make any contributions. The cost of this measure would be absorbed either by the government, which would make the contributions on their behalf, or by all contributors to the plan, as is now the case for financing the drop-out provision. Conditions could be attached to ensure that women (or men) who return to part-time or low-paying jobs receive the same assistance. Upon reaching retirement, they could choose the option that is most advantageous to them: either the exclusion of low-income years or the inclusion of childrearing years with credits equal to half the average industrial wage.

If this measure were adopted, there would have to be an element of retroactivity to cover those who have already raised a family and have not returned to the labour market. The principle of retroactivity can be justified very easily in their case; first, they are the group hit hardest by poverty and, second, the C/QPP already provide a certain degree of retroactivity to all contributors by paying maximum pensions after only 10 years of contributions.

Two other proposals seek to give explicit recognition to the social value of work done by women as mothers by giving them a personal monetary benefit.

■ Coverage of homemakers

It would not be difficult to implement proposals designed to acknowledge that women who raise children should not be penalized on retirement. On the other hand, attempts to define similar corrective measures for women who remain at home but have no children have encountered unforeseen difficulties.

185

The proposals are logically defensible. Housework is real work and provides a benefit to someone; those who do it should therefore be able to accumulate pension credits in their own name while they are doing it. Some have therefore proposed that anyone who claims a married exemption on his/her income tax return be obliged to contribute to the QPP or the CPP on behalf of his/her spouse. Single-parent family heads without employment income or with low income would also be eligible. These contributions, as well as those of people at home in low-income families, would be subsidized according to criteria to be established. Thus the proposal amounts to compulsory coverage of homemakers under the C/QPP. Its objective is to recognize the value of domestic work and to have the pension credits paid for by the person benefiting from that work, usually the husband.

The situation becomes complicated when we consider that domestic work is also done by women who have jobs and whose husbands do not claim a married exemption. Does that work have no value? What happens if the adult who keeps house is not a person for whom a married exemption can be taken, for example, if she is a common-law spouse, a mother, or a sister? What happens during a period of unemployment where two adults are at home? Because this proposal includes a specific method of financing (contributions based on whether the taxpayer takes a married exemption), it establishes discrimination based on marital status. Other proposals have tried to overcome this drawback.

- ■ Compulsory coverage of all adults, financed through a refundable tax credit

To circumvent the problem of discrimination, others have suggested that all adults, regardless of their status, be covered by the CPP or the QPP. The credits they accumulate would be fixed at half the average industrial wage. Because the proposal would cover people with no income of their own, a source of income must be found upon which contributions can be based. This would be possible if the current personal income tax exemption were converted to a refundable tax credit.

This proposal seeks to provide a decent retirement income to everyone. Its effect, however, would be to change the nature of the Canada Pension Plan and the Quebec Pension Plan. The purpose of these plans would no longer be to maintain a worker's previous standard of living relative to earned income but to give everyone a decent income in retirement. Is this not properly the role of Old Age Security and the Guaranteed Income Supplement?

Furthermore, if this reform were implemented, people currently without income of their own would probably have more immediate needs to meet with the refundable tax credit than paying contributions to the

186

C/QPP. As well, if people without income were required to contribute to an income replacement plan based in part on transfer payments, the plan might well become a savings plan, with each person receiving from it only what s/he had contributed, as is now the case with private plans.

The problem of poverty among retired people, particularly women, is one that needs a solution now, not a generation hence. The solution would not seem to be changing the basic intent of the C/QPP. Their objective is not to provide everyone with a decent income. This is, and should continue to be, the function of Old Age Security and the Guaranteed Income Supplement. The level of benefits delivered by these two programs should, however, be re-evaluated.

With regard to maintaining the standard of living of retired women, the solution lies in redefining the splitting rules within the C/QPP and in upgrading these plans. Recognition of the social value of raising children could be obtained through the adoption of a drop-in provision for people caring for their children under the age of seven, at a salary level deemed equal to at least half the average industrial wage, without contribution on their part. This could be done without entering a debate about defining homemakers, a drawback of other proposals.

Reform of Pensions for Surviving Spouses

The proposal for reform of the over-65 survivor pension is part of the demand for the automatic splitting of pension credits upon the retirement of the younger spouse. Since the pensions of the two spouses would be equal from then on, there would be no point in providing two options for calculating the pensions. Two proposals are generally made. The first proposal would apply in a system where housework would be recognized through the existing drop-out provision or a new drop-in provision where there are children under the age of seven, and where the credits are automatically split between the retired spouses. This proposal would allow the surviving spouse to keep 100% of his/her pension and to receive 60% of the deceased's pension. In this way, the surviving spouse would have a pension income equal to 80% of the couple's previous income. However, Old Age Security would not be paid to the deceased spouse, of course, which would leave the surviving spouse with less than 80% of the couple's previous total income.

The second proposal is usually advanced by those who propose that homemakers (for whom a married exemption is claimed) accumulate pension credits in their own name. Because these homemakers would have a higher retirement income under the proposal, the couple's income would also be higher. With credit-splitting on retirement, the proposal suggests that when one spouse dies, the surviving spouse would receive 100% of his/her own pension and 30% of the deceased's pension. Although this would correspond to 65% of the couple's previous pension income, that income would be higher because of the homemaker's credits. Some advocates of coverage for homemakers even go so far as to recommend abolishing survivor benefits. According to them, the existence of these benefits stems from the economically dependent status attributed to homemakers, but that situation would be corrected if homemakers were able to accumulate pension credits in their own name.

With regard to surviving spouse pensions for spouses under the age of 65, the problem is more complex. As noted previously, the amounts are low but they are paid over a long period of time, which explains why these pensions represent a large proportion of all payments out of the plan. The proposals most often advanced require a complete rethinking of the assistance given to surviving spouses, especially women. The younger the women, the more the solution lies in their re-entering the labour market. Some have therefore proposed that the surviving spouse benefits be much higher, but for shorter periods of time, defined in advance, to allow these women to re-enter the labour market or to upgrade their skills if necessary. This pension would be called a transitional pension and could be replaced, after a certain period of time, by a surviving spouse pension as we now know it, but at a lower level. This measure, however, could be of only limited value to more elderly women, who have been out of the labour market for a long time. Some thought must therefore be given to measures that would differ according to the age of surviving spouses or according to their degree of employability. There have seldom been precise figures attached to this proposal, but different groups have demanded that governments explore this avenue for a solution.

THE COST OF PROPOSALS

It is difficult to estimate the cost of these proposals precisely. One reason is that these programs are based partially or totally on transfer payments and, in that sense, are funded in various ways. One thing is certain. If society wants pensioners to receive better incomes, it must be accepted that this will involve transferring more income to them, whether through the tax system or through contributions to the C/QPP.

Governments have already announced increases in contributions to the C/QPP; they began in 1987 and will gradually bring the contribution rate to 4.6% by 1991. This increase will not mean any major improvement to the plan, however. It is justified solely by changes in current plan reserves and demographic changes in the population. The current reserves have stopped growing because more people are now drawing pensions. This is the normal result of the maturation of the plan. With regard to demographic change, the proportion of the population age 65 and over will continue to increase, with the result that pension benefits will have to be financed by the contributions of a smaller number of workers who are under the age of 65.

With the objective of maintaining reserves equivalent to two years of benefits, governments have tabled rate schedules covering the 25 years ending in 2011. This rate schedule must be revised every five years. Based on this schedule and the current benefits offered by the plans, it is predicted that contribution rates will reach 7.6% in 2011 (3.8% for the employer and 3.8% for the employee).

To estimate the increase in the cost of the plans resulting from the reform proposals discussed in this paper, the proposed level of benefits can be compared with current levels. Table 10.1 provides information on the current situation and some of the proposals.

Table 10.1   Comparison of Benefits:
Current Situation and Reform Proposals

	1986 Situation		Proposed Situation	
Universal Plans				
OAS	$3,420		That the total benefits	
GIS maximum			provided by these two	
■ single person	$4,067		programs be at least	
■ couple	$5,833		equal to the poverty line.	
Employment-related Plans				
			Replacement rate of 50% and	
One-income couple			automatic credit-splitting	
■ C/QPP, man	$5,800		man	$5,800
■ C/QPP, woman	$ 0		woman	$5,800
Surviving spouses over 65				
■ man (100% + 35%)	$5,800		man (100% + 60%)	$9,280
■ woman (60% + 60%)	$3,480		woman (100% + 60%)	$9,280

Some of the proposals made in this paper are very difficult to cost out. The proposal to allow exclusion from pension calculations of 25% or 30% of the worst years, for example, would mean that all those who do not already qualify for the maximum pension would see an increase in the pension payable to them. To establish a cost for this proposal, its effect on the average pension payable would have to be determined, which is impossible. In the same way, the proposal to allow pension credits, without contributions, for those who take care of children under the age of seven could only be quantified if the number of pensions that would be paid, as well as the transitional provisions that might be adopted, were known. However, the figures in the table show that if we want to improve the plans, we will have to pay more.

NOTES

1. This suggestion has been made by the Canadian Advisory Council on the Status of Women (March 1982), among others.

2. *Pension Benefits Standards Act,* section 27.

3. See, *inter alia,* the Canadian Advisory Council on the Status of Women's March 1983 Recommendation for the Elimination of Sex Discrimination With Respect to Pension Benefits.

4. This rate has been in effect since January 1, 1987. It was previously 3.6%.

5. The *Pension Benefits Standards Act* corrects this deficiency by guaranteeing entitlement to a pension after two years of participation in a plan.

6. Between 1966 and 1972, OAS was indexed by only 2% per year. After that, it was increased in line with consumer prices, except during the 6% and 5% control period.

7. Canadian Advisory Council on the Status of Women, *Planning Our Future — Do We Have to be Poor?* (Ottawa: 1986).

8. David A. Croll, *Poverty in Canada, Report of the Special Senate Committee on Poverty. Updating the Poverty Line — 1985.* (Ottawa: 1986).

9. As an example, on January 1, 1987, the maximum CPP pension for a surviving spouse under the age of 65 was $290.79 per month, while QPP pensions varied, according to age, from $438.52 to $506.39. The QPP orphan's benefits are $29.00 per month, non-indexed, while the CPP pays benefits of $94.79, indexed.

10. Canada, Health and Welfare Canada and Department of Finance, *Better Pensions for Canadians* (Ottawa: Supply and Services Canada, 1982); Canada, House of Commons, Special Committee on Pension Reform, *Report* (Ottawa: Supply and Services Canada, 1983); Québec, Ministre des Affaires sociales et Ministre de la Main-d'oeuvre et de la Sécurité du revenu, *Agir maintenant pour demain — une politique québécoise de sécurité du revenu à la retraite : énoncé d'orientation et plan d'action* (Quebec City: 1985).

11. See, *inter alia*, Coalition pour une retraite décente, *Manifeste pour une réforme des régimes de pensions* (Montreal: 1984). The coalition is made up of about 15 groups, including the FFQ, AFEAS, AQDR, YWCA, and Quebec union centrals.

The Canadian Advisory Council on the Status of Women was established as an independent advisory body in 1973 in response to a recommendation by the Royal Commission on the Status of Women. Its mandate, "to bring before the government and the public matters of interest and concern to women" and "to advise the Minister on such matters relating to the status of women as the Minister may refer to the Council for its consideration or as the Council may deem appropriate", is wide and may be interpreted to cover all Council activities on behalf of Canadian women.

The Council is an autonomous agency that reports to Parliament through the Minister Responsible for the Status of Women. This allows the Council to maintain a voice within Parliament and at the same time maintain the right to publish without ministerial consent.

The following were members of the Canadian Advisory Council on the Status of Women at the time of publication (September 1987):

Sylvia Gold
President
Ottawa, Ontario

Patricia Cooper
Vice-President
Calgary, Alberta

Clarisse Codère
Vice-President
Montreal, Quebec

Myriam B. Bernstein
Montreal, Quebec

Jacqueline Bissonnette-
Dulude
Montreal, Quebec

Erminie Joy Cohen
Saint John, N.B.

Jo-Ann Cugnet
North Battleford, Sask.

Héleyne D'Aigle
Edmundston, N.B.

Edith Daly
Montague, P.E.I.

Johanne Denis
Quebec City, Quebec

Emma Duncan-Kerr
Baie Comeau, Quebec

Lawrie Montague Edinboro
Chatham, Ontario

Barbara F. Fisher
Kincardine, Ontario

Margaret Fortier Delisle
Sillery, Quebec

Darlene Julianne Hincks
Regina, Saskatchewan

Veronica Mae Johnson
Dollard des Ormeaux, Que.

Robert McGavin
Toronto, Ontario

Linda Oliver
Halifax, Nova Scotia

Jane Pepino
Toronto, Ontario

Marie Daurice Perron
Hodgson, Manitoba

Cécile Rémillard-Beaudry
Winnipeg, Manitoba

Agnes Richard
Gander, Newfoundland

Peggy Ritcey
Riverport, Nova Scotia

Margaret Strongitharm
Nanaimo, B.C

Margaret Taylor
Believille, Ontario

Ann Tweddle
Edmonton, Alberta

Eva Voisey
Whale Cove, N.W.T.